"It takes a truly unique author to write a genuinely impactful book. Michigan Judge Rosemarie Aquilina is exactly that author. *Speak Up* is precisely that book. *Speak Up* will change the way you walk through your life and this world.

Major publishers will release almost 1,000,000 new books this year. *Speak Up* is a sure bet to sit atop that list because Judge Aquilina is 'one of one' and courageously pours herself and her unique life experiences onto the page in such a way that will inspire you and change you.

Rosemarie takes self-awareness to such an authentic level because she 'practices what she preaches' and by asking you thought-provoking questions that will ignite deep reflection, transform negativity into positivity, fears into productivity and failure into success.

I have known Rosemarie for many years and have come to respect her greatly and call her friend. She is unabashedly outspoken and captures the essence of how to reclaim and own your life, honor your own uniqueness and the goals and boundaries you set, without guilt or apology. *Speak Up* is a must read for anyone who feels stuck." — DR. PHIL MCGRAW

SPEAK UP

LESSONS IN
TRUSTING
YOUR
INSTINCTS

ROSEMARIE AQUILINA

BURMAN BOOKS
MEDIA CORP.

BURMAN BOOKS
MEDIA CORP.

Published 2025 by Gildan Media LLC, aka G&D Media
by arrangement with Burman Books Media Corp.
www.GandDmedia.com

SPEAK UP. Copyright © 2025 by Rosemarie Aquilina and
Burman Books Media Corp. All rights reserved.

No part of this book may be used, reproduced or transmitted in any manner whatsoever, by any means (electronic, photocopying, recording, or otherwise), without the prior written permission of the author, except in the case of brief quotations embodied in critical articles and reviews. No liability is assumed with respect to the use of the information contained within. Although every precaution has been taken, the author and publisher assume no liability for errors or omissions. Neither is any liability assumed for damages resulting from the use of the information contained herein.

Edited by Lara Petersen
Front and back cover photos by Emma Burcusel.
Book Design by Clarissa D'Costa

Library of Congress Cataloging-in-Publication Data is available upon request

ISBN: 978-1-7225-9922-5

10   9   8   7   6   5   4   3   2   1

*Dedicated to imperfectly perfect humans.
I see you. I stand with you. I celebrate you.
I support and encourage you and your journey.
Embrace change, joy, and positivity.
You're worth it!*

Contents

Introduction	9
CHAPTER 1: Confidence	11
CHAPTER 2: Relationships	23
CHAPTER 3: Fear & Fearlessness	37
CHAPTER 4: Trailblazing & Forging New Paths	49
CHAPTER 5: Bullying, Harassment & Intimidation	63
CHAPTER 6: Weaponized Incompetence, Ignorance & Indifference	75
CHAPTER 7: Imposter Syndrome, Honesty & Humility	91
CHAPTER 8: Integrity & Leadership	107

CONTENTS

CHAPTER 9:
Embrace Change With Voice & Choice — 119

CHAPTER 10:
Language Matters. Listen, Think, Speak — 131

CHAPTER 11:
Be The Insider In Your Life — 145

CHAPTER 12:
Success For You — 163

CHAPTER 13:
A Fully Assembled You — 177

CHAPTER 14:
Be Your Own Hero — 189

Final Thoughts — 201

Introduction

I testified before Canadian Parliament about making sports safe for all children, stating: "Safety is a complete sentence. It's not a question mark. It's a human right." After my testimony, Sanjay Burman approached me to write this book. I was flattered but wondered what he thought I had to say. I mulled over a plethora of topics and questions before I began writing. What are some of the lessons I've learned? What have I learned from others? What can I share that would resonate with others? Will what I've learned resonate with both men and women? Am I fully assembled enough to share what I've learned?

I reflected, and fourteen chapters emerged. Each one presents a thought-provoking question to encourage you to reflect on your life experiences, ignite the potential for personal growth, and better understand yourself and others.

I drew from my life experiences that came from motivational speaking, teaching for nearly forty years, and addressing various issues brought forward through employment, family, and friend matters. The situations in each chapter are very real, but I've changed names to protect the privacy of the individuals involved.

I am not a trained therapist, only an observer of life and human behavior. If you're struggling, there's no shame in seeking a trained therapist to talk with. Interview a few therapists to ensure you find one who is a good match for you: someone you can be open and honest with. Counseling is only as good as the honesty and openness that enter the room with you. There's strength in asking for help. It's empowering to take charge of your life, even when it's only by taking one small step at a time. Healing, learning, deciding, and making the right decisions for yourself takes time, and there is no time limit.

Be kind to yourself. The journey is long but worthwhile. The struggles are real but meaningful. The resulting joy of being the master of your life and the choices you make is bountiful, endless and contagious to others.

CHAPTER 1

Confidence

"Are you confident about your chances of success, or do you undermine your ability to succeed?"

Confidence is a state of mind. It's not something that some people have, and others don't. Everyone holds the key to unlocking their confidence and expressing it outwardly. It's not how many accolades, awards, or promotions one receives, and it's not defined by success and failure. Successful people can lack confidence, and people who fail can have confidence. A confident person's internal sense of self-assurance and capability sets them apart from someone who lacks confidence.

When you receive an accolade, and your first thought is to congratulate yourself for not messing up, you don't have confidence. The people who exude confidence are the ones who fail but don't punish themselves for it. They analyze their failures, reinvent themselves, and try again.

Having confidence and continuing to foster it, is like gifting yourself a superpower. This gift has the price tag of persistence, perseverance, and positivity, which costs nothing yet means everything. But, like any gift, it must be taken care of. Watch out for the people and things that can shake your confidence and destroy it.

Fear is the greatest enemy of confidence because it can mess with your head and make you doubt yourself. It's also a weapon others use against you because they're afraid you'll become better, stronger, or more successful than them. They can't fathom your ability to surpass them by accomplishing greater things than them or going places they've only dreamed of.

When you harness fear as part of your armor of assuredness, it becomes a powerful motivator for success. I was (and at times still am) fearful that I wouldn't be successful in what I wanted to achieve. I've used my fear of failure and turned it into my ever-present motivator. I turned my failures into teachable moments and chose not to listen to the naysayers. And while I listened to "advice," I chose which pieces of advice to consider and which to toss away. Through this process, I learned to always choose me and to trust my gut. With each success, I aimed at a new and higher goal, and with every failure, I analyzed, reinvented a plan, and pursued it. That has become a proven winning formula that has allowed me to remain focused, reach far beyond my goals and dreams, and achieve more than I thought was possible.

So, what's the difference between a confident person and someone who lives in fear and consistently undermines their abilities? Stated simply: one's outlook. A confident person understands that, to accomplish their goals, all they must do is to keep trying until they reach their goal. They know they don't have to succeed immediately, nor even the first, second, or tenth time around. They understand that they never fail until they quit trying. They also know, and I have learned, that maintaining a positive winning confident outlook is a necessary ingredient to the recipe of success.

The worst part is that failure leads to self-blame and losing confidence. Undermining your abilities tends to stop you from reinventing yourself and trying something different. A confident person stays positive and overcomes challenges. An intimidated person freezes and uses negativity as an excuse to quit.

Evaluating what went right and what went wrong is a starting point for nurturing a healthy sense of confidence. Planning effective strategies and integrating them into daily behaviors that slowly become habits builds a lifetime of self-reliance, self-assurance, and conviction, which results in the ability to exude confidence. Necessarily, this also includes time for self-care, during which you reboot, reconsider and retry, using setbacks, failures, or shortcomings, as teachable moments that catapult you forward.

You must understand that *you are enough*. You are deserving, and you have the right to be successful and to own that success. Confident people are proud of who they are and of what they do. They find happiness from within, and they're proud of their accomplishments—not what others think of them. Criticism does not bring them down; it prompts them to accomplish more.

Confidence is the ability to be who you want to be rather than comparing yourself to others or striving to be someone else. When you make comparisons, you're only limiting yourself. The ultimate empowerment comes from dedicating time to yourself and your goals. When you spend time comparing yourself to other people, you place limits on yourself by giving up your power and wasting time worrying about whether or not you measure up.

You have choices. You can choose to move forward and face your fears, or you can retreat into your fear. The anxiety and adrenalin that builds doubt and creates fear needs to be spun into an assessment that prepares you for the final run-through where you will achieve your goal. Flipping from a "can achieve" to a "will achieve" mindset changes the script from negative to positive. It reverses the pain of personal rejection or failure and turns it into a launching pad for success. The transformation is fraught with hiccups, hardships, and setbacks. Reworking your approach to a fresh mindset is an integral part of the journey. At times, you'll have no control over the barriers that lie ahead. Your only choice will be to move forward and own all of it but remember that each step you take builds strength and confidence.

People with confidence have developed the ability to listen and say no to the things they don't accept or don't want to do because they have nothing to prove. They take ownership of their decisions.

No is a complete sentence. It's not a negotiation. It's a way of honoring yourself and staying committed to your choices. Being wishy-washy, making excuses, or saying yes because you don't want to make waves doesn't honor you, your commitments, or your ability to choose for yourself.

When you listen to confident people talk, they speak with authority, conviction, and assuredness. They use phrases beginning with "I know…" or "I assure you that…" or "I'm certain that…" and stay away from uncertain phrases like "I think…" or "I'm guessing…" or other non-committing words. They're not afraid of being wrong and they're open to debate.

Confident people take chances because they have nothing to lose. They know their self-worth and draw it from within. Fear doesn't hold them back from achieving their goals. When the chance they took doesn't work out, they evaluate, reassess, and move forward with newfound knowledge, recognizing that setbacks inch them closer to their goals.

Asking for help, complimenting others on their accomplishments, and taking risks without fear of failure or reprisal are all signs of confidence. When you've mastered confidence building, you'll be comfortable with yourself and won't feel forced to conform or do what others want you to do. Concerning yourself with how others see you and worrying that taking risks will somehow make you seem weak or unintelligent are signs that self-worth and confidence are lacking.

Building confidence takes time, and a lot depends on what eroded it in the first place. Arlene spent years battling insecurity. Despite having beauty, a law degree, and charisma, she lacked a sense of confidence. I didn't know this about her when we first met, but it was something I discovered soon enough. I hired Arlene as an associate at my law firm because she had a unique ability to find the hidden gems that won cases. Her research and writing skills were impeccable and her excellent service to clients enabled me to double our clientele in no time.

The problem emerged after several months of preparing documents and serving as second chair on various cases alongside me and other attorneys in my firm. We all agreed Arlene was ready to represent client issues in court solo, so I assigned her hearings and trials that she would oversee and argue on her own, with our support, if needed. She very clearly said, "No!"

Arlene was afraid of making mistakes, not knowing the proper legal procedures, or how to respond to opposing counsel's objections and the judge's questions. She worried about soiling the firm's reputation. All I'd seen from her was stellar work, and I reinforced that she was a licensed, knowledgeable, well-versed attorney who was ready to shine. I held my position and advised our legal secretary to schedule her accordingly.

When the day came for her to prepare for hearings, she found a pile of files on her desk, along with the upcoming client and court schedule. Arlene approached me, files in hand, and said she couldn't do it. I was prepared for this reaction. I handed her the schedule book, which clearly showed that everyone else was booked and those were her cases—end of story. She locked herself away in her office and cried for an hour before buzzing the legal secretary. Arlene asked her to organize the first file for the upcoming motion and let the client know where to meet her in the courthouse.

Arlene didn't know I had a hearing in the next courtroom. I'd timed everything so I could sneak in while she was arguing the motion in preparation of trial. I saw her walk up to the podium, file in hand. Even from behind her, I could see her confidence growing with each sentence and nod of the judge's head. She was articulate, focused, and every bit the professional she needed to be. Arlene won the motion and returned to counsel table and sat next to her smiling client with her head held high. She'd faced her fear and was radiating confidence.

While Arlene was always over-prepared, her confidence grew exponentially every time she went to court, attended mediation, or had a conversation with an opposing attorney. Today, Arlene is a very well-respected attorney. While she tends to be timid about touting her many accomplishments, she no longer questions her abilities or worries about what anyone will think about her.

Confidence is a teachable skill that I pass along to my students. In every trial class I teach, I require each student to stand up and practice the part of the trial they just learned about. These skills include demonstrating knowledge and proficiency in making an opening statement, doing direct and cross-examination, arguing motions and responses to objections, conducting jury *voir dire*, and finally, a closing argument. I grade students on the record they make, their overall performance and a final trial. While most of these students want to be trial attorneys, a few don't, yet they recognize the need to challenge themselves to feel more confident about their ability to practice law and chose the trial track to embed the confidence needed to practice law overall.

Gail was a student in my trial class. She never intended to enter a courtroom, but she compared herself to her zealous trial-bound classmates and felt inadequate, unworthy, and scared that she'd never measure up as a lawyer in any capacity. Despite having excellent grades by the end of her first year of law school, Gail lacked the confidence to recite cases or debate and answer her professors' questions in front of the entire class without trembling. She suffered from stress migraines, had nightmares about failing and refused to join a study group because she felt she was so much farther behind than her peers. Upon the recommendation of her counselor, she applied for the trial track and was one of only thirty-two accepted out of over 150 applicants.

After the first day of class, Gail asked me to please not to call on her first, explaining she hoped to never argue in court. I agreed that, initially, I wouldn't, but eventually everyone had to take their turn at being first, including her. She winced and silently nodded. Just over the halfway point of the semester, six weeks before the fully graded *voir dire* and trial, I asked Gail to perform her closing argument. Throughout class, we were in a mock courtroom. I asked students to sit in the jury seats so they would understand the jurors' perspective of what was said, heard and seen.

Gail stood. She faced her jury of classmates and eyes down, began reading what she'd written. I stopped her and asked her to stop reading her notes and do her best from memory. Gail cried and began shaking. She said she couldn't, and that it didn't matter because she'd never have to argue before a jury. I disagreed. She'd done the work. She was prepared. She would perform.

I asked each juror student to turn their chair around, so they faced the back wall. I explained to Gail that no one was watching her. She could do it. Although she cried, she eventually took a deep breath and began. She didn't use her notes and delivered a compelling closing argument. Once she was finished, her classmates turned around and cheered. Through her tears, she grinned and stopped shaking and crying. She'd faced her fear, and it boosted her confidence.

Gail never again asked not to go first, nor did she shake or cry during mock trial practice or the final graded full trial. She sailed through the rest of the course and the graded trial and passed with top grades. Gail is practicing law and doesn't hesitate to go into the courtroom. She is a mentor to students who, like her, just need a small push to expand their goals and realize that pushing past their fear plants a foundation of confidence that never stops growing.

Confidence is something you can acquire and improve over time. It's a process that involves making a conscious decision to recognize and own your self-worth. It comes from being clear about your abilities, choices, and goals with such certainty that you own them without explanation or apology.

When you project confidence, others perceive you as competent. Confidence has a ripple effect that touches everyone you interact with. The catch is, you can't fake confidence when you know absolutely nothing about what you're asserting. Having confidence in your words and actions, without undermining your worth, knowledge, or experience, helps you earn credibility and allows you to move forward without fear. It's important to note that being confidently competent doesn't mean you put others down or imply that they're incompetent. By lifting yourself up and others along with you, you establish yourself as a credible leader who people will want to connect with socially and professionally.

CHAPTER TWO

Relationships

"Are my relationships positive and empowering, or negative and limiting?"

Relationships are difficult to maintain, but they're part of life and can have positive or negative aspects. Some people are meant to be in your life forever, and others serve their purpose before moving on. Being in a relationship isn't limited to the realm of romance or intimacy, but includes acquaintances, family, friendships, and work or situational connections. Overlaps occur when you work closely with someone you're married to or in an intimate relationship with. Despite your best efforts, some relationships become toxic and threaten your emotional and physical well-being. Knowing when to stay and when to leave is often difficult, but it becomes easier when you understand the importance of prioritizing yourself over others.

A relationship is defined by the connection you share with another person; however, the best, first, and most important relationship to maintain is the one with yourself. You must nurture a positive internal image of yourself and a positive outlook. Sounds like common sense, doesn't it? It might even sound like rhetoric.

Think about all your relationships—those with people who support you and those who undermine you. Who ghosted, groomed, gaslighted, or discouraged you? Who has been there to encourage and motivate you, and will continue to be there for you through both joys and struggles?

By developing self-trust, self-confidence and self-assurance, you can attract and maintain strong, positive relationships with similarly confident and positive people. When considering the relationship you have with yourself, understand that being your best self is not only a service to yourself, but one that positively serves everyone you engage with. The relationship you have with yourself should be the most honest and supportive one you have. You need to be your own best friend before you can be in a supporting role. To engage in meaningful relationships with others, you must first be self-aware, self-reliant, self-prepared, have self-love and self-acceptance while taking proper care of yourself. None of these acts are selfish; however, all are necessary.

There's an enormous difference between selfishness and self-awareness. A selfish person is egocentric and needs to be the focus of attention, even when it seems they're trying to be empathetic or helpful. Selfish people take, rarely give, and are incapable of putting anyone else's needs first. Self-aware people are in tune with their needs and feelings, and they honor their love for themselves. They understand that showing up for themselves is showing up for others and that saying "no" helps them become a better person instead of a resentful one.

There's a healthy balance between recognizing your own inherent worth and value, and still being willing to provide meaningful help and support to others, even if that help occasionally requires some personal sacrifice to your emotional or physical wellbeing. It's not selfish to prioritize yourself or your needs, or to set boundaries and expect others to respect them.

Taking care of your own needs doesn't equate to selfishness, because you can still demonstrate that you are sensitive to the needs of others. Breaking into a habit of self-care is healthy and you have every right to acknowledge that navigating your own life is important. There will always be times when you need to concentrate on yourself. It's equally important to recognize when other people's needs must be prioritized. Acknowledging and accommodating those needs sets you apart from a selfish person, because those actions demonstrate that you're a keenly self-aware person.

To build an intuitive, strong relationship with yourself and others, you must learn to listen to your heart and trust your gut. Even the best relationships are always difficult. There's no question or issue with that—it's a proven fact. Enjoying a good relationship with yourself can be taxing when inconsistencies, emotion, and sometimes logic get twisted, or when what you want doesn't align with what you have. Managing relationships takes a lot of work, patience, and acceptance from the parties in the relationship, and it doesn't matter if it's a dating, work, family, or friend relationship. What matters is having the fortitude to walk away and choose yourself when a relationship becomes toxic.

Shelley's story serves as a perfect example of finding the strength to walk away from a soured relationship. She worked on a project with me, and I found her to be brilliant, kind, and well educated. I appreciated her patience and intellect, and I let her know it. I commented positively on her abilities, sense of humor, and her joyful laughter. She was overly grateful and wondered how I could possibly see any of those things in her. I suspected something was weighing on her because, despite her jovial demeanor, her expression was often sullen.

Shelley expressed how disappointed and upset she was with herself. It surprised her that I saw her as a positive person when she felt so negative about everything in her life. What surprised her most was that I could see that she carried a heavy burden.

I asked Shelley if I could help her with anything, even if it was only to lend an ear. No judgment, just a safe space for her to talk and me to listen. Shelley nodded and, without looking me in the eye, said that she'd broken up with a longtime boyfriend several months earlier. She was so upset about the loss that she gained weight, quit her full-time job, and fell into a deep depression.

When she felt better, she began seeing people again and found someone she thought was worthy of dating. Let's call him Dick. After a few months, Shelley discovered Dick was very much like her previous boyfriend, but worse. Dick was cheating on her with one of her best friends. She was hoping to change him and win him back and blamed the whole situation on her girlfriend.

I left Shelley shocked and speechless when I told her she deserved better from her "best friend" and boyfriend. Her jaw literally dropped, and her eyes popped open wide. I told her she didn't have to agree with me, but I suggested she answer a few questions to fully understand what I meant before making up her mind about her relationships.

Although I'm not a therapist, I have a lot of common sense, and I've dealt with all kinds of people from all walks of life in all sorts of capacities. From my varied experiences, I developed a series of questions I use to determine which people I want to include in my life and which I refuse to allow into it. I promised Shelley that I'd only ask the questions I thought were relevant to her situation, and then asked her to answer with only the first words that came to mind. She agreed. Here are the questions I asked and her responses:

Q: Did he show up on time for your dates?
A: Never.

Q: Did he cancel often or invite you out at the last minute?
A: Often.

Q: Did he pay, or make excuses for you to pay?
A: I paid for a lot.

Q: Was he able to hold a stable job?
A: No.

Q: Did he have a felony record?
A: Yes, but he told me he only pled guilty because he got such a good deal that he didn't want to risk going to prison. He didn't commit a crime; it was only self-defense.

Q: Did he listen while you shared your feelings, without judgment?
A: No. He constantly interrupted me when I spoke. He made me feel guilty for my flaws and shortcomings. He said that he was the only man who would ever love me because I occasionally smoke cigarettes and I'm fat.

Q: Could you be yourself in the relationship?
A: I tried, but not really.

Q: Did you feel you had equal power in the relationship?
A: Never.

Q: Did you feel unsupported, demeaned, angry, and depressed when you were with him?
A: (Shelley gulped hard and didn't blink.) Yes, but I felt I did something wrong. I tried harder to please him.

Q: Did you give more than you got from the relationship?
A: Yes. (She paused.) Always.

Q: Did he ever compare you to other people?
A: Yes, especially when we watched television.

Q: Did you talk about the future together and how it would work?
A: I tried, but he'd accuse me of pressuring him, and then change the subject.

Q: Did he ever compliment you?
A: He liked that I held a job, was a hard worker and kept busy.

Q: Did you have higher self-esteem and self-assurance before you met him?
A: Absolutely.

Shelley had always known the answers, but speaking them aloud with someone she trusted made her situation real. It was daunting to realize how much time and money she'd wasted on yet another man who didn't appreciate her.

I dug a bit deeper by asking if she had any friends or family who gave her as much as she gave them. Her only answer was, "My father." Her siblings and the few friends she had could always count on her, but when she needed help, they were too busy.

Shelley recalled getting a flat tire when she was on her way to make dinner for her father. After repeatedly asking her siblings for a ride, or to bring their father dinner, Shelley ended up riding with the tow-truck driver to the tire store, where she found out she had to get a rim replaced and buy four new tires. She paid for an Uber to take her to her father's home, then a second Uber to get home, and then a third one in the morning to return to the tire store.

Since Shelley's friends and family were almost always too busy to lend a helping hand, she asked what she should do. She felt lost, so we made a plan. To begin, Shelley needed to learn to appreciate herself and acknowledge her qualities and abilities. To do that, she needed to make herself a priority first. Although helping people was deeply ingrained in her identity, she had to establish boundaries and honor herself by limiting how much she did for others.

Shelley hesitated to agree with the plan and said, "Everyone will be mad at me. I'll be alone."

And there it was. Her real obstacle: Fear. Fear of taking control and moving forward with her life. Fear of standing up for herself. Fear of getting to know herself. Fear of rejection. Fear of being alone. Fear of being unable to find a mutually beneficial relationship.

Shelley thought it was easier to spend her valuable time on others instead of herself. Avoiding her nagging gut and silencing her doubts and fears was easier than facing the risk of failure. It was easier for her to work more and share her income with a man who loved her money than to refuse him and deal with the guilt when he left. Seeing herself through the eyes of those around her, Shelley decided she was an unworthy failure who had to work harder and prioritize others over herself. From my perspective, those people weren't worthy of having her in their lives, and I let her know it.

Once Shelley learned to respect herself and prioritize her own needs, others would follow suit, regardless of the relationship she had with them. Those who truly loved and respected her would remain in her life, and those who didn't would leave.

I suggested Shelley find a therapist. Perhaps not right away, but maybe when she felt ready for a new relationship. A therapist could be her "secret-keeper" and life-skills cheerleader until she could be that for herself.

Meanwhile, we crafted a list of her positive attributes and the things she liked to do and the things she didn't. What emerged was a tangible list of her goals and dreams and a concrete plan for attaining them.

At first, Shelley was shy about saying anything good about herself, so I chimed in with all the valuable attributes I saw in her. Shelley wrote the list in her own handwriting so she could see it, internalized it, and have an easier time recalling it. I asked her to post it on her bathroom mirror, read it daily, and then add one positive note each day along with a self-care activity.

Shelley needed to internalize and reflect on her value and learn to appreciate how much she mattered and how important her needs were. She was valuable on her own without being attached to a man. I suggested that, before getting involved with someone new, she take the time to learn about herself, be clear about what she wanted, practice saying no and asking for what she needed. She needed a best-friend relationship with herself.

Shelley called me several months later. After our chat, she took the time to clear her head and work on herself. She committed to walking for an hour every day, no matter the weather. On her walks, she carried her cell phone and dictated notes. When she returned from her walk, she transferred the important points onto a sticky note and stuck it on her bathroom mirror. Eventually, she had notes on the wall around her mirror, the back of her bedroom door, and all over her apartment. She used them as a roadmap to understand and discover her true self in all aspects.

Shelley found a good therapist and lost fifty-eight pounds. Although she has a few more to go, she's getting asked out on dates but has so far declined each one. She reconnected with a few friends from high school and college and made a few new ones at work. She's working on letting go of feeling like she must be needed in order to feel valuable. Today, Shelley is happier than she's ever been, and she considers herself her best friend.

Each type of relationship comes with its own unique nuance. It's important to look at what's happening in the relationship—not the ways you can fix it. Not all relationships are meant to last, and trying to repair them beyond their expiration date is frustrating and depleting, and usually results in an unnecessary bitter end.

There have been people in my life who I considered friends, only to discover our friendship had run its course. Peggy and I had known each other since high school, although we didn't go to the same school or events. We were never close, but our parents were. I saw her a few times during our college years, and she attended my wedding.

Life happened, and we found ourselves living in different states, but our parents remained close friends. For over thirty years, I looked forward to seeing Peggy every summer and enjoyed catching up. We got together to play cards, have coffee, take walks, or enjoy the sun at the pool with our children.

A few years ago, much to my surprise, Peggy stopped talking to me. At first, I thought it was my imagination, but it became apparent when she avoided me at the pool. Her response to my greetings was a stiff "hello" and she would look away when we found ourselves in the same store or restaurant. She stopped using the pool and instead claimed a stake beachside.

Convinced there was a problem, I sent her a text and asked if I had somehow offended her. She replied, "Of course not." However, Peggy hasn't spoken to me since, and she acts like I'm not in the area when she sees me, even when we're standing a few feet apart, talking to the same group of people who do engage positively with me.

Ghosting in friendships isn't a unique situation. When relationships end, it's easy to blame yourself or wonder what you did or should have done or shift the blame onto the other person. How you handle the situation is a choice.

When someone is upset with me, I don't take that on. Rather, I recognize that it's their issue, not mine. I refuse to carry another person's baggage, especially after I've confronted the situation head-on, and there's a denial that contradicts my visceral gut reaction to being treated like that. I choose *myself*. I stand with *myself*. I honor the relationship with myself.

I focus my energy on positivity and free myself from accepting blame or taking responsibility. The relationship I have with myself begins with self-trust and being able to live with my choices. I am the one who decides who to keep in my life and who to let go of. I choose to keep solid friendships and I value my few true friends.

The world is a big place, and people will enter and exit your life for various reasons. Your time and energy go to waste if you spend too much of it contemplating those reasons. The key to being my own best friend is keeping my power and cultivating positivity within myself.

While every relationship is unique, you must value yourself to be valued. That takes effort, and it begins with working on your mindset every day. Believe in yourself on the good ones *and* the bad ones. Be strong enough to walk away from anyone who doesn't respect you. You deserve kindness, positivity, and to be with someone who supports and uplifts you.

Comparing yourself to others or being compared to others is unfair, and it's detrimental to your self-worth. You are special simply by being your unique self. In any relationship, both parties should recognize each other's individual distinctiveness, strengths and weaknesses, and always promote well-being. Prioritizing open communication, honesty, mutual respect, and a desire to work out differences are all important to maintaining positive relationships. The key to maintaining your emotional well-being is letting go of the people who ignore you or treat you unkindly.

Putting yourself first and striking a healthy balance between having a positive outlook and a caring relationship with yourself will diminish any feelings of selfishness. You'll know when you've reached that balance when you release yourself of any guilt, inadequacy, or shame for choosing your needs ahead of others. What you'll find in place of all the negativity is inner peace, joy, and overall well-being. What you'll reap are honored boundaries, mutual respect, and honest, harmonious camaraderie.

CHAPTER THREE

Fear & Fearlessness

"Am I stuck because of my fears, or am I willing to bravely move past them and toward opportunity and success?"

The broad definition of fearlessness is *being without fear*, but there is so much more to the meaning of that one-word concept. The meaning and application of fearlessness encompass bravery, tenacity, moxie, and valor. These attributes are important to recognize because there are infinite ways to be fearless, act with courage, and live in confidence.

No one is fearless because fear is a necessity for survival; however, when you live in fear, you're not living with purpose—you're living in pain that immobilizes you and prevents you from living a joyous, fruitful life. Fear is the door to opportunity and success when you use it to motivate yourself into action, even if that action leads to failure. Every failure moves you forward. Each failure is a moment to grow, adjust, and redirect your efforts toward reaching your goal.

Why do we use the term *fearlessness* when, technically, in its purest form, *being without fear* doesn't exist? Because we need to recognize, understand, and face our fears to conquer them. We either rule our fears, or they rule us.

Fearlessness drives success by eliminating self-doubt, self-pity, and fear. Being fearless doesn't mean living without fear, because fear is a guidepost to intuition and gut feelings that warn you to be concerned and cautious. Good fears are warnings; bad fears are limitations. Being in a state of constant fear means it's taking control of your life and choices.

While sensing fear is synonymous with trusting your inner gut and recognizing warning signs of danger, it's also an instructive tool that will lead you to safety and success. Understanding the value of fear and the teachable moments it offers is priceless. Simply stated: fear is the door to success.

Fearlessness is about pushing past the things that make you feel uncomfortable and challenging yourself to become your best self. It doesn't mean going skydiving when you're ill-equipped to do so and have no real desire to try it. It means applying for a job you want despite feeling unqualified or good enough. It's accepting your fears, learning to analyze what the catalyst of each fear is, and accepting that they don't have to rule your life. Fear doesn't have power over your choices, and with the proper perspective, you can put fear in its proper place. Realizing that you are your greatest gift is a powerful step toward conquering your fears and living fearlessly.

Fearlessness empowers you to move forward, leave uncertainty behind, and then act in your best interest, uninhibited by doubt. This isn't to say you don't have doubt. It means you discount it and choose yourself and your goals over your fears. When you're successful, confidence swiftly replaces doubt and fear. You soar higher and go farther than you ever imagined possible.

As you embark on the journey of understanding your fear and learning to be fearless, stay focused, remain positive, and pay attention to the vibrations you emit into the universe, both intentionally and unintentionally. What you put out into the universe, you get back. It really is that simple. In fact, there's a direct link between confidence and competence, and being fearless.

At times, I've walked into a room and instantly felt a wave of intellectual prowess emanating from the people around me, and I thought, "Wow, everyone in this room is smarter than me. What have I got to offer?" In those circumstances, I usually head for the buffet table or make a beeline toward someone I know. I take a few minutes, listen carefully, and reflect on my knowledge, worth, and inner strength, and then I'll push myself forward.

At an opportune moment, I'll join a conversation and add a comment, ask a question, or give a compliment. When I speak, I use a kind but confident tone while making eye contact with the people I'm talking to. Without fail, I'm brought into the conversation in a meaningful way. Within minutes, I feel in control, competent, and equally worthy of being there.

I faced my fear. I *am* fearless. This is not an anomaly. The key to success in all things, big and small, is in understanding and overcoming fear, benefiting from those teachable moments, trusting your gut, and then choosing to live fearlessly.

Having the courage to express who you are on the inside and communicate what you need and want is one of the greatest gifts you can give yourself. This requires that you consider, understand, recognize, and own your vulnerabilities, which allow you to be your authentic self. Embracing vulnerability, without being too modest or condescending toward yourself, is a courageous act that will catapult you toward fearlessness, fulfillment, and owning your power.

The act of being fearless fosters vulnerability. Being vulnerable doesn't mean you're weak. In fact, dissecting vulnerability reveals inner strength and the power to overcome the limitations imposed by your past. When a person feels vulnerable, it means they're in touch with their inner needs, which include their strengths, weaknesses, and desires.

Pursuing your dreams can feel daunting when fear starts to creep in. Never give up pursuing your dreams. Stop breaking promises to yourself, and instead pursue the commitments you made to yourself while maintaining a winning spirit. Amid discourse, adversity, and uncertainty, find the courage to honor your dreams. By confidently staying the course, you will realize your full potential without allowing fear to limit you.

Understand that you are worthy and never discount yourself. Give yourself permission to take all the time you need. You own yourself and you have every right to do so. In other words, you don't need permission to spend your time on yourself.

I want to inspire you with a story about a woman I know who learned to chase her dreams with absolute fearlessness. Angela was thriving in her position at a large manufacturing company. She was certain she was about to be promoted to vice president of marketing—until self-doubt crept in. Her ideas were being shunned at several strategy meetings, only to be reassembled by a male teammate, and then accepted as brilliant. She debated whether to speak up and thank them for adopting her original ideas, as reintroduced by her colleague, but worried that her interjection would jeopardize her opportunity for promotion.

Outside of the boardroom, Angela spoke to a superior who recognized her contributions and advised her to step up next time and take the credit that was rightfully hers. He said, "After all, when you're a VP, you'll have to make those tough calls and promote your worth." Angela felt the sting of his words because she knew he was right.

A few months later, while Angela was still awaiting the promised promotion, she received an inquiry from a headhunter who was interested in setting her up for an interview with a competitor. The job was also for a vice president of marketing. An internal promotion created an opening for the job, and the hiring committee was seeking someone with Angela's skill level to take on the role. The opportunity intrigued Angela because it offered a $25,000 salary increase and an additional week of paid vacation, so she agreed to the interview.

Fearful of getting fired, Angela didn't use the competitor's interview as an opportunity to remind her bosses of the promotion and raise she'd been waiting for. She worried about disrupting her work-family balance, leaving her coworker family, and being able to work with the same skill set at another company. She feared that, by not attending the interview, she would give up what might be her only shot at moving her career forward.

The interview was only a few days away, so Angela did what she did best and researched the company, the position, and the person who last held it. She compiled a binder to showcase her achievements, awards, "attagirl" notes, letters, and thank-you cards. Angela's fear pushed her into being over-prepared.

Four people made up the interview panel. She firmly shook the interviewers' hands and greeted each one with a smile. Before sitting down, she laid the binder in the center of the table. While one interviewer looked through the binder, another went ahead with the questions.

As the interview progressed, Angela wondered when the trick questions would come up, or when the difficult ones would surface. She eased into answering questions and quickly realized that her preparedness had given her the strength, confidence, and freedom to be herself. Angela realized she was enough and banished her fears. She knew that if she wanted the job, it was hers.

When they offered her the job, under the terms the headhunter had outlined, Angela gulped. She heard her superior's voice telling her to promote her worth. Either she had the job, or she didn't. She decided she had nothing to lose and advocated for herself, demanding her full value.

Angela held her breath for a moment and reminded herself that she was about to go down a scary path, but not taking it would be even scarier. "According to my research, the previous vice president of marketing was a male, and he started at $40,000 more than what you're offering me. I am worth the same salary and, over time, I'll prove that I'm worth even more."

All four panel members were stunned and asked her for a week to see if they could get approval for the higher salary. One interviewer commented that he respected her forthrightness, honesty, and research. He shook her hand and expressed his desire to work with her.

Angela got the job offer *and* the salary she wanted. Her former employer apologized for underestimating her value and said they would gladly hire her back if she ever wanted to return to the company.

Ultimately, Angela pushed past her fears and fearlessly moved forward with courage, conviction, and a victorious voice. Today, Angela no longer cares what others think of her. When she acknowledged her value and overcame her fear of failure, she discovered a renewed sense of freedom.

Angela's former superior's wise words stuck with her, and she shares them with her own subordinates when they need inspiration or a boost in confidence. In her new role, Angela's fearlessness has seen a ripple effect move through her team. Through a positive and cohesive approach, they have earned multiple team awards, while she has received numerous leadership accolades. Angela no longer gives in to her fear. Instead, she moves past it and turns it into success.

During that same time, a brand-new lawyer, Dan, had a jury trial almost immediately upon beginning his practice. He'd been in front of me a few times prior and had a habit of clicking his pen, which not only distracted me, but annoyed my court reporter, who relied on her sharp hearing to do her job.

Each time I saw a click pen in his hand, I asked him to approach, ordered him to swap his pen for one of my non-clicking pens, and reminded him about the distraction.

He said that clicking his pen absorbed his fear of public speaking, and he promised he would get better.

I assured Dan that he didn't need the pen. On one occasion, he began his opening statement using hand gestures for emphasis. And then I heard it. I saw it. The clicking pen.

I never interrupt opening statements, so I waited. Dan made a pause for emphasis and, without thinking, stuck the pen in his mouth. In a matter of seconds, dark blue ink was dripping down his chin. I asked him to approach, handed him a wad of tissue and pointed to his pen.

Dan looked down and realized his hand was stained with ink. We then paused for a recess. Before we returned to the record, Dan asked if I would continue the trial later in the afternoon or the next day. Opposing counsel shrugged and had no opinion; however, I declined. I advised Dan to use the mishap to his advantage. There were a lot of ways to face his fears, and this was one of them.

When the jury returned, Dan's hands were stained blue. Washing his face caused the ink to smear all over his face, and he had smudges on his shirt. With no pen in hand, Dan began with a smile. He lifted his hands and turned his head, allowing all fourteen jurors to see his ear-to-ear grin.

"Ladies and gentlemen of the jury," he began, "what you see on me are blue ink stains. You see, I feel so passionately that the evidence in this case will prove the innocence of my client, that my pen broke. As you listen to the facts and evidence in this case, I want you to ask yourself if there's enough credible evidence to lead you to believe beyond a reasonable doubt that he is guilty of the charges. Look at my face. Although there's a lot of blue ink, I am not fully covered in blue. *Beyond a reasonable doubt* doesn't mean beyond *all* doubt. It requires that the proof and evidence presented by the prosecution, who bears the burden, is so convincing that there is no other explanation. But ladies and gentlemen, as you listen to this case unfold, and then when you go into the jury room, think of my face and the parts that aren't covered in blue ink. If you decide there are portions in this case that aren't covered in blue ink, so to speak, you must find the defendant not guilty."

Dan faced his embarrassment and his fears. He fearlessly connected with the jury in a unique way, using the situation to his advantage, and he won. He no longer uses click pens and has overcome his fear of public speaking by recalling the exploding pen incident.

Dan conquered his fears and moved forward by facing the scarier thing: failure. Dan's fear of losing a case and disappointing himself and his clients was overwhelming. He challenged himself to not let his inner fear hold him back. Despite his fear, he took the more daunting path because not taking it was scarier. By challenging himself to work through the uncomfortableness, he learned he was capable, strong, resilient, and competent.

When you let your fears control you, you answer to them and remain paralyzed in an uncomfortable state. But when you face them, you take control and move forward with greater ease. Focus on your future and face your fears so you can choose yourself and experience the joy it brings. The only one standing in your way is you. Don't hide in the darkness. Seize the opportunity to grow and become the beacon of light you were meant to be. Shine on yourself and share your light with others.

CHAPTER FOUR

Trailblazing & Forging New Paths

*"Do I follow worn paths without question, or
do I trust my instincts and create my own path?"*

It's personal circumstances that often forge your path, not desire. Feeling disconnected from yourself can make veering onto an uncharted path seem impossible or impracticable. The fear of change stems mostly from criticism and self-imposed roadblocks.

Taking the time for self-care and self-evaluation is key to determining whether you should stay the course or veer off and change direction. Evaluating yourself can be difficult. Take your time. Make a list of where you are, where you want to be, what you want to accomplish, and how close or far away you are from achieving your goals. Keep adding the behaviors, people, and circumstances that stifle your ability to choose your course.

Finally, make a list of what you need to succeed and evaluate whether you're determined to work hard to achieve your goals. If you need help, find a therapist, life coach, or mentor you trust and can be honest with. And make sure they support your goals. Naysayers aren't allowed inside your trust circle. You are the driver of this mission, and you must act with valor, drive, and purpose to promote your ultimate goals.

Know your value. Be authentically you. Don't ask for permission. Don't be smaller just to allow other people around you to be bigger. Assert your right to live, develop, and travel on your unique path. Enjoy putting your talents and gifts to good use. Your unique vision forges a path that is entirely your own.

Commit to your plan, goal, or idea. Stand tall and forge a new path without apology, explanation, or deviation. Never compromise your goals, worth, or belief in yourself. Every new path is a valuable opportunity to transform the ordinary into the extraordinary and problems into solutions.

You *are* enough. Pave the road to *yes* and avoid the road to *no* without regret or deviation. When life throws you an unexpected detour, understand that it happened *for* you, not *to* you. Enjoy the new adventure and all its teachable moments. Your choices, instincts, and self-belief are the building blocks for forging new paths that will shape you into your best and most powerful self. And if you choose to stay on a solid, well-worn path, that too is superb.

Choosing the road less traveled with the goal of fulfilling your dreams to the fullest might involve making choices that go against the expectations of family, friends, employers, or religious and cultural communities. You may face scrutiny, shame, isolation, or even bullying. The most critical outcome is learning to say yes to yourself. Recognize that your contribution is valuable. The upshot here is trusting your gut, intuition, and intelligence. Appreciate that roadblocks, detours, and the struggles of creating a new path will expand your world and produce beautiful, infinite possibilities.

The first step in forging a new path is to adjust your outlook on life, similar to how you would adjust the rearview mirror in your vehicle before driving. Start by being your own champion. Surround yourself with people who encourage and mentor you and support your goals. But don't wait for those people to appear, because they may never show up.

Your journey, like each fingerprint, is unique. You own it, and it's your opportunity to embellish the mark you make on the world. There's no one-size-fits-all formula for finding your happiness and being your authentic self. Everyone has the right to embark on that journey and discover who they are and who they want to become.

When people try to discourage you, shake up your beliefs, or interfere with your journey, stay on the path with greater conviction. Trust yourself, and never let anyone see—not even for a split second—that they've shaken you. Understand that you don't need any external reassurance, encouragement, or motivation to plod forward.

Cast off others' doubts and keep going. Remind yourself that you haven't asked permission to fit in, nor is that your intention.

Your goal is to excel and be your best self in the manner that exudes who you are. Stay focused on your new goals, the adventure, and building something from your perspective. Hard work, vigilance, and intuition will guide you and reward you when you follow your own path. You won't experience satisfaction or fulfillment if you take the well-worn path. That journey will not excite you, fulfill your true self, or catapult your aspirations.

Pursue your own passion instead of doing what others think you should do. Let the doubters speak to themselves while you cast off their negativities. Challenge yourself to accomplish more, visualize your destination, and explore any detours that emerge along the way. These revelations might be the most important ones you'll ever consider. Take the time you need to reflect and contemplate your options. Remember that every journey has surprises, and you have the right to change direction, leverage your talents, develop new skills, and make different choices. Armor-up and be prepared to plunge past the forks in the road with a determination that maximizes your momentum and focuses on success.

Don't allow heat from criticism, doubt, or discouragement to deter you from pursuing your dreams. There will always be negativity. Be who you are. Be vigilant and know that there are far more resources than threats, but you need to be aware of both. It's the experiences you have, both good and bad, that shape who you are—not the opportunities you missed. Failures and setbacks are teachable moments, and the only real failure is not trying. There's always a way to refocus and accomplish meaningful goals and ambitions if you stay true to your authentic self, not the person others think you should be.

Overcoming adversity builds self-assurance and inner strength, which is essential for growth and success. Confidence and strength are tools in your inner toolbox that help you cultivate instinctive endurance, overcome obstacles, and move forward with a sense of hope instead of dwelling in despair. The finest gift you can give yourself is a meaningful life, driven by your wants and needs, and filled with the happiness and sense of accomplishment you deserve.

While new paths can be lonely, and even frustrating at times, supportive people will join you on your journey. They provide clarity and increase your conviction. When forging a new path, it's rewarding and often life changing when you accept all the bumps and bruises along the way as part of the learning adventure.

Eventually, like-minded visionary people will become your allies and you'll find strengths and resources you didn't realize were available. You'll rise above the naysayers who had no intention of supporting you, regardless of your goals. You'll find innovation, satisfaction, and growth in ways you never thought possible. Ultimately, you will come to the realization that you possess resilience, resourcefulness, and the skill to transform challenges into opportunities.

On the first day of class, I always ask each student to introduce themselves and tell me where they're from, why they took my trial class, and what kind of law they hoped to practice. I was in awe of a beautiful, graceful, intelligent student in my class, Jennifer. Although she looked familiar, I couldn't place her.

I make sure students get the most out of my class, and knowing a little about them helps me to be a more effective and relatable teacher. Jennifer was from California, and she wanted to be a trial attorney in the military. I offered to help her since I had served in the Judge Advocate General's Corps (JAG) for twenty years.

I teach my trial classes in a mock courtroom. Every week, I have all students on their feet practicing various parts of a trial while those watching sit in the jury box. I offer feedback and the students practice until they master the task at hand. Some students can quickly reset their performance, while others have to work harder at it.

Jennifer grasped my comments, adapted, and not only improved her skills but also showed potential to become a superstar lawyer. Jennifer stayed after class one evening to have a conversation with me. I'm always happy to mentor my students, so we sat together, and I listened. Bright-blue-eyed Jennifer was usually confident, but she slumped in the chair across from me. "The other students said the delivery of my opening was over the top and I'm too flamboyant. What do I do about that?" she asked, her voice cracking and her eyes watering. "Am I really that bad?"

And I responded, "Jennifer, I wish they were all like you. They wish they were you. It's clear to me that you'll be the attorney to watch, the attorney who connects best with the jury, and the attorney who makes an outstanding record."

Jennifer jerked her head and shoulders back and upright. "Really?"

"Really," I stated with emphasis. "Being a lawyer is a bit like being an actor. You must connect with the room and present solid arguments, facts, and law in plain language and in a manner the jury can understand, relate to, and remember. Your opening statement did all of that and more. You have a unique and memorable style that comes across as knowledgeable and confident." I met Jennifer's eyes. "Have you had acting lessons or performed in high school plays?"

Jennifer nodded. "I've been in a few films. I'm using the money I earned, along with the scholarship I received, to pay for law school. After hearing the students' comments, I'm considering moving back home and returning to acting, but that's not my dream. Being an attorney is."

"I'm proud of you for having the courage to confide in me and ask for help, and the confidence to display your skills in front of your classmates. I guarantee you will be among the top attorneys within a few years of practice. Your acting skills make you shine. Don't listen to the naysayer wannabes. You're the one to watch, not criticize."

"I'm not over the top? I mean, my presentation . . . it wasn't too much?" Jennifer knitted her brow.

"Absolutely not. Don't listen to them. Listen to your inner voice and trust your intuition. You chose to switch paths to forge a new one by listening to your gut. There will always be criticism. Trust your instinct."

"My instinct is telling me to run back to California where I have work waiting for me," Jennifer said.

"Being a lawyer means advocating for your client. But you must first learn to advocate for yourself. In every career path, there will be people who want to tear you down. Every lawyer has faced criticism. Your preparedness, instinct, and talent will help you succeed. Stay true to your path and don't let others define you, shake your confidence, or change who you want to be. Promise?"

"Promise," Jennifer said, her voice carrying a new sense of conviction.

Jennifer earned and received the Outstanding Student award that term. It was an interesting term because, as it continued, she received less criticism from the other students, and some of them began emulating her style.

She married a classmate, and now they have two beautiful children. She fulfilled her dream of becoming a JAG officer and had multiple offers from law firms before graduation. With steady promotions in the firm she works for, Jennifer has become the superstar lawyer I always believed she would be.

When I was a district court judge, I was assigned to a specialty court. Sobriety Court is designed for defendants who need treatment in lieu of jail because of a drug and/or alcohol addiction. It's an intense court with four phases and immediate sanctions if the defendant is noncompliant. Sanctions can include jail time or an increase in treatment. That's when I met Kyle. He pleaded guilty and was sentenced after being arrested for drunk driving for the third time, which is a felony punishable by up to five years' incarceration, loss of driver's license, and other sanctions. On the date of the offense, Kyle's high blood-alcohol content indicated that he was an alcoholic, even without a substance-abuse assessment. He entered sobriety court with the understanding that his felony would be reduced to a one-year misdemeanor after graduation. Treatment included four phases, ranging from minimal requirements to extremely intense requirements that had to be completed within two years.

Kyle lost his sales job because he lost his license and couldn't drive. Because his vehicle had been impounded, he sold it and bought a bicycle. He chose not to contest his divorce and received supervised parenting time until he completed substance abuse treatment and satisfied the court that he no longer used or abused substances. Before and after his scheduled time with his daughter, he had to take a breathalyzer test.

Determined to reinvent himself, Kyle entered intensive outpatient treatment, attended alcoholics anonymous (AA) regularly, and found a sponsor. He moved into a residence that was on a bus line to court, treatment, and AA meetings, and within walking distance of his daughter's school. He then found a job within biking distance. Although it wasn't his dream job, Kyle took the barista position because the experience brought him closer to his goal of owning his own business. Running a coffee shop chain had been on his wish list since entering business school, but he never pursued it after graduation.

Kyle evaluated the obstacles and realized that, instead of dealing with his marital issues, he and his ex-wife had avoided them by wasting their disposable income on booze and taking lavish vacations. He regretted all those things but was determined to break free from that lifestyle and get back on the path he'd been on when he was in high school and college.

The reality of going to prison and losing the right to raise his daughter was a huge wake-up call. Kyle recognized that the destructive path he was on was unacceptable. He looked at the situation as something that was happening *for* him, not *to* him, and used it as a learning experience to confront the stress and disappointments he'd previously numbed with alcohol.

With a renewed sense of commitment to himself, Kyle veered off the path of destruction and onto a path that promoted his best self. He wanted to be a proper father figure and someone his daughter would look up to and be proud of. Admittedly, Kyle had a lot of work to do.

Following a fifteen-month journey, Kyle graduated from Sobriety Court. He completed everything without having to be sanctioned. At his graduation, his then eight-year-old daughter told him she'd always loved him, but now she liked him, too. Once he'd earned unsupervised parenting time, Kyle walked her to and from school on his days. They spent quality time together every day.

Eventually, Kyle's daughter made a few comments about her mother that caused him to suspect his ex-wife had fallen into an all-too-familiar pattern. She'd found a new boyfriend, and they were drinking too much. Kyle had a hunch that Mom and the boyfriend left the daughter alone while she was asleep to smoke weed or leave to buy more alcohol. His ex also started dropping their daughter off at odd times, and if Kyle wasn't available, either set of grandparents took care of her.

He was extremely upset and texted me, fearful of going back to court because he was certain the judge wouldn't believe him. Kyle didn't know how much more fight was left in him, so I explained that he had a choice to make. If he did nothing, the worst outcome (besides his child getting hurt) would be losing his daughter to foster care if his parents or his ex-wife's parents didn't take her. He despised the idea and vehemently declared that he would never allow it.

Kyle dipped into his savings account and hired a lawyer. He had to postpone his dream of owning a coffee shop to take the path that involved fighting for custody. Keenly aware that he hadn't yet been clean and sober for five years, Kyle attended more meetings and found a second sponsor. Regardless of the outcome, he knew the court battle would be a heart-wrenching experience because it involved the person he loved most in the world, his daughter.

After months of documentation and hearings, Kyle was finally awarded sole physical custody. And after five years of not having a driver's license, he finally got his back. Kyle bought a vehicle and found a partner to invest in a coffee shop chain, and they made concrete plans to purchase a second one within five years. His daughter often does her homework at a reserved table at the coffee shop, and she wants to work there when she turns sixteen. His ex-wife now has supervised parenting time, which will continue until she decides to choose her child over her addiction and enter residential treatment.

Kyle took the time to evaluate himself and his life's journey. Now he sees everything clearly and holds himself accountable. He remains a proud and humble man who understands that every misstep paved the way to the productive path he's on now. Kyle achieved more than he thought possible. He learned to respect himself and thus earned the respect of his child. Priceless.

It takes a backbone to do something you haven't done before—like confronting naysayers, seeing infinite possibilities when others see only the impossible, overcoming obstacles, or starting out fresh. Having a backbone means being curious, persistent, and patient enough to focus and learn from experience. Find mentors and experts, ask questions, and explore answers that align with your goals. Show up every day for yourself and focus on reinvention, innovation, and the transformation of failures into triumphs.

Regardless of what happens, believe in yourself, your plan, and who you are inside. Your unique journey will be filled with surprises—including the potential for failure—but it's your mindset and actions that make all the difference. Your willingness to forge a new path and be a trailblazer already makes you a success. The journey is in front of you. It's reachable, and it's yours for the taking.

CHAPTER FIVE

Bullying, Harassment & Intimidation

"Am I being controlled, or am I in control of my life?"

People often use bullying, harassment, and intimidation interchangeably, but they have distinct and important differences. The consequence of each is the infliction of serious, long-term psychological harm on the bully's prey. These intentional acts can be virtual, written, verbal, or physical. What they have in common is that they interfere with a person's right to feel safe. These behaviors have the power to disrupt a person's life, relationships, education, livelihood, and freedom of movement. Some victims fear that damage to their personal property or reputation will be so severe that they suffer long-term mental health disorders, which can include physical ailments.

Bullying refers to intentional acts of unwanted, aggressive, and dominant behavior aimed at a victim the bully perceives as weak or vulnerable. Bullies intend to cause psychological, social, or physical harm by making threats, spreading rumors, or purposefully excluding someone from a group or function. Bullying can happen once or multiple times, and it involves real or perceived imbalances of power. Acts of verbal and physical abuse can occur within familiar relationships, not just with strangers. It can happen anywhere, including online, at school, or in the workplace, and can occur in almost any form, including by text, email, social media platforms, involvement of third parties, or instant messaging.

Posting or threatening to post revenge porn or other personal photos or information can lead to identity theft and public humiliation. Being targeted by a bully can cause stress, embarrassment, fear, anger, and vulnerability. A victim's isolation and inability to seek help can lead them to exhibit negative behaviors, and in extreme cases, suicide.

There is no justification for bullying. While it's often difficult to understand the reasons for a bully's behavior, it can help the victim purge the feeling that they somehow brought on or deserve the attacks by understanding that the bully has unresolved personal or social anxiety or was a victim of bullying themselves.

Harassment is any act that causes harm to someone's physical or mental well-being, either directly, overtly, or through a third person. The most common types of harassment are discriminatory and sexual.

Discriminatory harassment happens when someone is repeatedly subjected to offensive conduct because the victim engaged in a protected activity, or because of their membership in a legally protected class, which includes race, color, ethnicity, religion, gender, sexual orientation, national origin, age, disability, or socioeconomic status.

Sexual harassment involves unwelcome sexual statements, advances, and requests for sexual favors. It also encompasses unwanted verbal or physical conduct based on the victim's gender. The harasser sometimes threatens to harm the victim's reputation, employment, or community standing if they don't fulfill sexual demands. Those who engage in sexual harassment create negative and hostile working, educational, or family relationships.

Intimidation refers to conduct designed to provoke fear or anxiety. It can be subtle or overt, but the intent is to gain an advantage over the other person. Sometimes, intimidation involves explicit or implicit threats of bodily harm, property loss or injury to a pet or a loved one.

In some cases, aggressive behaviors are not deemed bullying, harassment, or intimidation. Examples include:

Acts of self-defense or defending others: This refers to situations where people use aggression to protect themselves or others from harm.

Law enforcement interrogations: Aggressive questioning techniques employed by law enforcement officials during interrogations can be justified in certain circumstances.

Parental discipline within acceptable limits: This acknowledges that certain forms of discipline are acceptable, as long as they don't cross into child abuse.

Negotiation tactics using legitimate claims: Aggressive tactics may be employed during negotiations to assert one's position or interests, as long as they are based on legitimate claims.

Competitive contexts: Aggression in sports, business, legislative matters, or legal/court matters may be used strategically to gain a competitive advantage.

Constructive feedback in the workplace: Providing feedback that may be perceived as aggressive can be used to motivate employees to work harder or meet deadlines.

Recognizing when you're being intimidated can be difficult, and admitting it is even harder. Intimidation in any form, under any name, is an abuse of power. Intimidators commonly inflict emotional damage on their victims, and in more severe instances, even physical abuse.

Feelings of intimidation can lead to low self-esteem, helplessness, and social anxiety. When people feel intimidated, they sometimes stop doing their best work or being their authentic self, and then find themselves in a cycle of unhappiness, negativity, and despair.

Intimidation *can* be used for good reasons, such as outsmarting an attacker or protecting children from harm. However, it's often used for harmful reasons like gaslighting or grooming. Absent a lawful reason, intimidators and bullies have no moral right to overpower another person. Although their power appears formidable, in reality, it is flimsy and flawed. The key to unraveling their perceived power is to name the lying, deceit, cheating, and weaknesses, and then cite the truth to the intimidator and any coconspirators. Understand that anyone who enables inappropriate behavior is a coconspirator and must be confronted with the truth.

It's important to call intimidators out to successfully erode the dominance they project. What is equally important is to stand with victims when you see this happening. If you are the target, gather allies to stand with you. By choosing to stay out of the fray or turning a blind eye to bad behavior, by inference, you condone the malicious behavior, which makes you a coconspirator. This is not to say you should place yourself in danger. Instead, trust your gut and ask law enforcement or someone in authority over the intimidator for help. Depending on the situation, ask them to assist, intervene, or protect the targeted individual.

Intimidators count on inflicting emotional damage on their victims and those around them. The psychological damage is immense; however, when someone stands up, intervenes, and supports the bullied individual, it makes a positive impact on the victim's self-perception and their outlook on the world. Intimidators and bullies don't expect their victims to report them, talk back, or call them out.

When someone attempts to exert power and control over you, focus on what you can control: your reaction and response. Bullies and intimidators have likely been victims of bullying and intimidation, so they respond by mirroring the actions that were done to them. No matter how badly a person has been bullied, their experience is no excuse to pass it on to someone else. When you intentionally take part in intimidation of any kind just because you have a history of being intimidated, you give up your personal power. Instead of asking for help or support, you're allowing fear to control you, and you're losing your power and dignity in the process.

With this understanding of bullying, harassment, and intimidation in mind, think about your own experiences. Ask yourself if you've ever intentionally or unintentionally used bullying, harassment, or intimidation to obtain results, and then reflect on an instance where you were on the receiving end of those behaviors. Consider the circumstances of each situation. Did you need help dealing with any residual effects? Asking for help and seeking treatment is a sign of inner strength. You have a right to be happy, secure, and safe.

The moment their indefensible actions and behaviors are called into question, people who bully, harass, or intimidate are unmasked as cowards. If you're a victim, remember that you are not the problem. The problem is with the bully, and the only way they know how to release their trauma and pain is to project the same feelings onto others so they can turn their weakness into power.

That backwards thinking of bullies is part of how they developed a skewed vision of themselves. By seeking help or treatment, or by taking action against their perpetrator, they could have begun the healing process. They could have turned their pain into power to be used for good—not for inflicting pain on others.

Tara and Jim were victims of these behaviors. They were a young married couple who jointly owned a business with Rick and his son, Paul. The business thrived until the economy changed. While profits were still good, instead of considering solutions, Rick blamed Tara and Jim, who recently became parents. Rick bullied them into investing more money into the business. They did so just to keep the peace and put an end to the taunting.

Rick accused them of not putting enough time into the business because they were more focused on the baby. The additional money Jim invested didn't stop the harassing calls or bullying comments. In fact, it seemed to make things worse. Jim made it clear the partnership was over and proposed a buyout.

They agreed to a price, and Rick and Paul became the new owners. Over the next few years, the business remained stable, but it couldn't sustain itself. Rick, who was the majority owner, closed the business and filed for personal bankruptcy.

After leaving their company, Jim got an executive job in an auto company and was doing very well. Tara was a stay-at-home mom and had recently been diagnosed with an aggressive form of cancer. When it became clear that Rick's business was on a downward spiral, he frequently showed up at Tara and Jim's home. He blamed them for the business's failure, accused them of stealing, and demanded money. It didn't make sense to Rick that his former business partners were doing so well while he was stuck dealing with a failing business and bankruptcy.

Rick often spoke with a loud voice that carried a rude tone, all while keeping his fists clenched. When Jim left the room, even for just a few seconds, Rick took advantage of his absence and made hushed sexual remarks to Tara, claiming he could satisfy her in ways her husband never could. Thereafter, whenever she found herself alone with Rick, Tara immediately excused herself and locked herself in the toddler's bedroom.

At first, she thought she misunderstood the things Rick said, and then she began blaming herself. She finally told her husband what was happening, and Jim immediately installed cameras and stopped responding to Rick altogether. They blocked his numbers and social media connections and stopped associating with their mutual friends. Everything seemed to calm down; however, Tara's cancer had spread, which shifted their focus and completely changed their lives.

Several months later, while Tara was spending her last few days at home with comfort care in place, cars lined up in the cul-de-sac where they lived. One after another, men kept showing up at their door, ringing the doorbell at all hours, claiming they were responding to an ad. The men were causing such a disturbance that their neighbors called the police.

What Jim and Tara learned was that someone had placed an ad on the dark web inviting men to have sex with Tara, claiming they needed the money because of her illness. The ad listed prices for various lewd acts and noted that Jim consented and liked to watch.

Detectives immediately got involved and linked the ads to Rick, who faced civil and criminal charges. In the civil case, he was found responsible, and Jim was awarded a multi-million-dollar judgment. Rick was also found guilty of multiple counts in the criminal charges against him and ordered to pay restitution. Sadly, Tara passed away during the proceedings, and it's unlikely that Rick will ever pay the restitution or the civil judgment against him.

Rick used all three negative tactics against Jim and Tara. His antics not only affected him, but also had a negative impact on his son, business, and reputation. After serving his prison sentence, it was almost impossible to find meaningful work. Most of his friends and family members stopped associating with him. Those who still kept in touch with him no longer trusted him and refused to recommend him for employment.

Once you engage in such harmful behaviors, you compromise yourself and unleash a ripple effect that can quickly escalate beyond your control. It's always best to take the higher road, maintain your power, and stay honest like Jim and Tara did. Playing the blame game or employing bullying, intimidation, and harassment tactics is always a losing strategy. Instead, take charge, surpass your fears, and rise above intimidation. This approach keeps you strong, balanced, and focused, and transforms your fear into confidence.

Even with the #MeToo movement and substantial court settlements, there's been minimal accountability or change in the persistence of sexual harassment and sexism. While cases of harassment in the educational and workplace environments have been somewhat curtailed, demands for safer spaces and better reporting systems are constant and necessary. While the goal is to report and eradicate all incidents, that isn't always possible. On multiple occasions, I have been the target of harassment. I'll name just a few.

While in practice, an attorney made a comment about how I looked and asked if my husband gave me permission to leave the house and practice law. I responded to the male lawyer by asking if he would like to repeat that question in front of the State Bar Attorney Grievance Commission. He never attacked me again.

During law school, I got married and had two children. I was tired, busy, and overworked, and I quickly lost the pregnancy weight I'd gained. One afternoon, when I was sitting on the steps of the law school reading cases during my coffee break, a professor leaned over and whispered in a deep and disturbing voice: "How does it feel to have all the men looking at you again?"

After the shock settled in, I replied: "How will it feel when I repeat your words to the dean?" He never approached me again.

Early in my pregnancy with the twins, I was at risk of losing them, so I had only told a few people I was expecting. The Chief Judge called me, saying that he heard I needed a lot of time off work. When I told him I didn't know what he was talking about, he revealed that he knew I was pregnant.

I asked him if he knew something my doctor hadn't told me. I then advised him that I didn't have the luxury of taking maternity leave when my other children were born, and that I'd follow my doctor's orders, not his. He quickly backpedaled and told me I could take all the time I needed. I told him I didn't need his permission to take time off and ended the conversation.

I reported this male Chief Judge and stood with other female judges who had also reported him. Not one person, nor entity in power to assist with the bullying against me and other judges, ever took the bullying seriously or followed through with the help that was promised; however, the Chief Judge was eventually forced to retire.

Harassment of all kinds is rampant on the bench. Although I and other female judges have asked for help over the years, there has been no follow through to date, only empty promises of action and training. Some female judges retired sooner than they planned, fearful of the continued emotional toll on them, understanding that change was not on the horizon and there was, nor would there be, any viable acknowledgment that they'd been heard.

I tell you this because you are not alone. Everyone in every profession is susceptible to bullying, intimidation, and harassment. The first step in addressing the issue is to hold on to your power and prioritize yourself. Know that you did nothing wrong. Solutions exist. Documenting and asking for help or pressing charges is also important. Base your decision on what you can emotionally handle and what you want to achieve. Seek counseling if you feel overwhelmed.

CHAPTER SIX

Weaponized Incompetence, Ignorance & Indifference

"Am I in a healthy, happy relationship that supports and encourages me to be my authentic self, or am I being held back?"

It's no accident that this chapter immediately follows the one on bullying, harassment, and intimidation, nor is it duplicative. Although there are similarities, the upcoming topics shed light on the global perspective of our complex relationships with others and ourselves, making them equally worthy of discussion. Understanding the impact of weaponized incompetence, indifference, and ignorance is key to unlocking your power to fighting fear and making informed decisions. It is also important to recognize that incompetence, indifference, and ignorance can emerge in any type of relationship, not just romantic ones. It can infiltrate peer groups and immediate family relationships. Therefore, when thinking about these concepts, don't limit your analysis. Instead, think about all your relationships.

Weaponized incompetence is a recent term that encompasses a willful power imbalance (a type of controlled bullying) and unacceptable passive-aggressive behavior. It happens when one person claims to be unable to perform a task, which forces the other person to do it. Although the behavior can be inadvertent, once someone realizes what they're doing and deliberately continues doing it, it ceases to be accidental and becomes strategic.

It's possible that some people were conditioned to use weaponized incompetence during childhood. When children witness their mother taking on the bulk of the household responsibilities while their father earns the income, that normalizes the power imbalance, which the children then replicate when they set up their own households.

Weaponized incompetence can also be intentional in a way that seems complimentary but is really a strategy to shift the workload. For example: "You are a better cook than me, so you should prepare all the holiday meals," or "You're a better speaker than me, so you should do the presentation before the board."

Weaponized incompetence can manifest in any relationship, such as at home, at work, among family members, or between students working on a "team" project, etc. The result is always the same: an imbalance of responsibility, a lack of accountability, a power shift, or the "team" taking credit for one person's work. It's a strategic approach that places most of the work on one party, even if they deny it or make excuses.

Indifference, ignorance, and incompetence are related to weaponized incompetence behaviors in the same way arrogance and control are related to one another. They create a lethal cocktail that condones and eventually normalizes unacceptable behavior. Often the victim becomes so entrenched in the grooming and gaslighting behavior that they fail to recognize the imbalance. Grooming is any behavior that a predator uses to gain trust and then an advantage over their prey. Gaslighting occurs when a predator deliberately causes a victim to question what they know to be true by feeding them inaccurate information and/or challenging their self-esteem. Once the victim recognizes this behavior, they often feel guilty over getting involved, or they believe they did something to deserve it. Sometimes they choose to ignore the problem rather than acknowledge what happened. Victims can become so entrenched in the relationship they believe they had that they harbor feelings of guilt and pity for the predator. They refuse to or struggle to take action against their bully, or to simply walk away.

Weaponized incompetence is at the heart of the breakdown of many relationships. It's a clear but unspoken message that the person feigning inability intends to shift the responsibility onto the other person so they can get out of performing undesirable tasks. When it works, they are free to do more of what they want while simultaneously taking that freedom away from the other person. This strategy leads to resentment, stress, and a sense of being unseen, unheard, and undervalued. It impedes communication and erodes trust and equality in a relationship. When the behavior persists, extreme cases of weaponized incompetence can cause severe emotional trauma.

Quite often, when the overburdened partner tries to train, shift, or trade responsibilities to correct the imbalance, the other person takes offense. Any attempt to have a meaningful discussion results in the controlling partner guilting and/or gaslighting the victim into believing they are crazy, wrong, or unappreciative. The controlling person may retaliate with: "If you think you're so great, you do it all." This is a form of deception they use to perpetuate their destructive behavior and maintain power and control.

In healthy relationships, there's a balance of give and take. Open, honest communication is fostered through trust and respect among the people in the relationship. They don't resort to telling lies, gaslighting, grooming, or ghosting when problems arise.

There are multiple ways to recognize weaponized incompetence. Trusting your intuition is paramount in any relationship to avoid getting trapped in a relationship where you are the target of incompetence, indifference, and ignorance. Falling into that trap results in accepting more responsibility simply because it's easier to do it all yourself than to put an additional strain on the relationship. Those who witness this pattern of behavior and encourage the instigator are coconspirators.

To evaluate the state of your relationships, ask yourself key questions to ensure each one is healthy. For example, are you exercising patience when teaching your children how to perform household chores? When they're old enough to help, do you begin by training them in the "teamwork" approach, and then teach and assign them age-appropriate tasks?

Roommates can split chores, responsibilities, and costs when they develop ground rules, but how will those rules change when one roommate is unavailable for an extended time?

Should couples discuss sharing the responsibilities before or after walking down the aisle? Before or after moving in together? How will the couple share those responsibilities once they start a family? Putting this discussion off or not following through with agreed-upon responsibilities is a red flag that can fuel anger or create distance between partners.

Professional relationships can be properly managed through regular meetings and asking questions. An employee can look at their job description, work assignments, and meet with their supervisor. Similarly, students should be able to refer to a detailed syllabus and meet with the assigning teacher when they need clarification or help with allocating the workload on joint projects and assignments.

Whatever the relationship, there are ways to manage tasks, give credit where it's due, and maintain a give-and-take balance, but it takes work. Know your worth and don't worry about not being well-liked. When people don't seem to respect you, it's enough that you respect yourself. Eventually, others will catch on and follow your example. Your actions will resonate with those people who can't speak up for themselves.

By asking yourself simple questions, you can evaluate the strain on your relationships. Remember, you put your happiness at risk if you don't answer truthfully. You can place any type of relationship or place a specific person's name in the "my partner" portion, as appropriate.

- Is there a noticeable pattern of behavior developing between my partner and me?
- Does my partner claim to be incapable of performing a common task that most people can do?
- Does my partner ask to be taught how to perform tasks, or help me when I take tasks over?
- Does my partner fake an illness to get out of performing tasks?
- Does my partner complain about sharing responsibilities?

- Does my partner claim to be too busy or tired to take on some extra responsibilities?
- Does my partner shift responsibility to me simply because I'm never as busy as they are?
- Does my partner claim that every time they perform a task, I redo it or complain?
- Does my partner claim I do a better job performing a task, and therefore I should always do it?
- Do I feel valued or burdened by this relationship?
- Does my partner ever ask if I need help and then follow through with helping me?
- Does my partner ease my burden when it becomes too much for me?
- Does my partner collaborate with me, or only cause a fight and leave me to do all the work?
- Do I feel anxious when I ask my partner for help?
- Can my partner and I agree on a fair division of tasks without arguing?
- Other than sharing the workload, are there other aspects of the relationship that are imbalanced?
- Do I resent my partner for not helping?
- Does my partner resent me for expecting their help?

Feigning ignorance is a tactic for weaponized incompetence. Ignorance is simply a lack of knowledge or understanding because you haven't had the opportunity to learn about it through formal education or life experiences. There are different forms of ignorance.

Willful ignorance is deliberately choosing not to be informed about a particular topic.

Factual ignorance is the lack of knowledge about critical facts, like how many continents are in the world.

Deep ignorance is an unwillingness to consider evidence or consider alternative perspectives, or to update your knowledge in light of new information.

Object ignorance is the lack of experience with a specific object, like never having operated a forklift.

Technical ignorance is being unfamiliar with specialized subjects, systems, or processes, or accepting it without fully grasping how it works.

Undecided ignorance is when someone cannot decide whether to learn or stay in a state of limbo.

Complete ignorance is the lack of cognitive abilities to understand concepts owing to age, mental illness, or a disability, etc.

Self-deception is a common form of willful ignorance. It occurs when individuals choose to believe falsehoods with such conviction that they genuinely deceive themselves, even in the face of contradictory evidence.

No human knows everything; therefore, there's humility in acknowledging that you don't know what you don't know and offering to learn what you need to know. These critical moments define your character and strength, or lack of it. A strong person investigates and asks for help, while a weak person feigns expertise and lives in a state of ignorant arrogance while trying to manipulate, deceive, and control others.

Ignorance is no excuse to feign competence. When you don't know something, it's important to be honest and accountable, and that motivates you to educate yourself. Failure to use ignorance as an opportunity to learn erodes trust, promotes incompetence, and demonstrates a lack of respect for yourself and others. Once someone who feigns knowledge realizes people believe them, they often become lazy and incorporate their tactics into a normalized routine.

Being indifferent means, you lack sympathy, interest, or concern for yourself, others, or your community. A relationship is bound to fail once indifference seeps in because respect and care diminish, making it highly unlikely that the partners can salvage their connection.

Numerous warning signs indicate that indifference is becoming a problem. It can start with even the smallest unresolved disagreement or when one partner doesn't feel heard. Signs will vary depending on the relationship, but they can include a lack of physical and/or emotional intimacy, a loss of curiosity about the other partner's interests, and failure to celebrate the little things. This can lead to dismissing holidays and other memorable occasions like birthdays and anniversaries and spending less time together. Communication breaks down and what might have been thoughtful responses turn into caustic responses like: "Okay," "Whatever," "Sure," "Anything you want," "I don't care," and "You figure it out." What emerges is dishonesty, infidelity, and patterns of lying or omitting vital information.

Indifference can be repaired and even foster stronger, harmonious bonds, but it takes constant effort, even after you've resolved the issues that once divided you. When faced with new difficulties, constant vigilance forges a resilient and unshakeable bond; however, early intervention and mutual effort are integral to saving a relationship plagued by indifference. Without due diligence, the relationship is not only doomed to fail, but remaining cordial may not even be possible.

If you're feeling uncertain about your partner, ask yourself if indifference has crept into your relationship. If it has, you're probably wondering if you should break it off or try to fix it. When you care about each other enough, there are steps you can take to repair the relationship, but it takes hard work, compromise, and a willingness to share the blame. You'll have to set aside indifference, anger, and resentment. This struggle is real, but worthwhile. And if the relationship doesn't work out despite your efforts, at least you both know you gave it your best. And, if the relationship breakdown is with a family member, it is even more important to recognize the issues, keep trying and working on repairing what divides you.

Both sides should feel comfortable sharing their feelings and experiences without fear of personal attacks or hostility. They should discuss when they believe the indifference began and why it began and what caused it to persist. The objective is to achieve a mutual understanding without adding arrogance or attributing blame, but rather by acknowledging that both parties are at fault and there is a mutual willingness to make changes. If arrogance or hostility arises in conversations, consider seeing a professional therapist who can help you work through relationship issues and develop a plan to identify and overcome them, so they don't divide you further.

Identify patterns of positive and negative behaviors, likes and dislikes, and then agree on a plan to change the pattern. Throughout the process, there must be a genuine commitment to persevere, acknowledging that your relationship may not be the same as it was before, but it will be stronger, worth keeping and nurturing.

Beginning anew with a stronger bond must include participating in the events you once loved doing together. Keep the list of likes that you made nearby so you can refer to it daily. Compare schedules and commit to going on dates. In between those dates, add a few new activities that either or both of you want to try. Honesty, patience and communication are the key ingredients to the positive survival of any meaningful relationship.

By incorporating activities that align with personal or shared goals, you can strengthen your understanding and support for one other. These events don't have to be elaborate, expensive, or time consuming. However, they must provide an opportunity to enjoy quality time together that also incorporates time to relax and engage in conversation. Bake a pizza with inventive toppings you both like. Try a new recipe or restaurant. Listen to an audiobook together. Open yourself up to a new movie experience by trying out a different genre. Join a couples yoga class. Go for a walk or a bike ride. Watch Bob Ross and paint a picture together or take classes. Note that these activities are not limited to continued bonding with your partner, they work well with anyone you love. Spend quality time with your children, siblings, or other loved ones you feel out of touch with, or continue strengthening the bonds you have. It provides time for building trust, opening communication and creating lasting positive memories.

When you have ideas for activities, jot them down and toss them in a hat. Pull them out in random order and then fit them into your calendar, with a commitment to not change or cancel plans. Whether it's a new experience or a repeat, keep it enjoyable and effortless, not a burden or duty. Show up with the same enthusiasm and willingness to engage as you did when the relationship was fresh.

If you're unable to reconcile your differences or find a shared starting point, therapy can help you move forward. Seek a qualified therapist with experience in couples or family counseling and has additional training dealing with trauma. Referrals from reliable doctors and other trusted sources can help you find the right person. Ensure that you have trust and compatibility with your chosen therapist, as raw honesty is vital for effective therapy.

Sometimes relationships run their course and simply come to an end. Regardless of whether the separation is permanent or temporary, it will hopefully end on a positive note, leaving any angst or animosity behind. If that isn't possible, seek professional help because emotional baggage is a heavy burden that can affect your physical and mental wellbeing. Ruminating over failed or distanced relationships is a heavy burden to carry alone.

Whether you realize it or not, residual emotional baggage can permeate new or existing relationships, and the overwhelming odds are that it will eventually cause problems. Take the time you need to heal. Residual emotional trauma can develop into weaponized incompetence, ignorance, or indifference. Individual therapy, or even a retreat focused on healing, may help you reignite the most important relationship you'll ever have—the one with yourself.

When I was married, my husband claimed his hands were too big to change diapers. He also regularly brought home the wrong groceries and couldn't fold laundry properly. Out of frustration and a need to get those and other tasks accomplished, I started doing everything myself. Conversations left me frustrated and I became increasingly unhappy. At times, I was so busy and sleep deprived that I didn't have time to consider the root of the problem. I didn't feel I could ask for help. I felt like an incompetent, unorganized wife, and I kept trying to reinvent myself and find ways to accomplish everything without asking for help. When I couldn't, that became part of the reason I eventually left my marriage.

Simply stated: I resented that the marital "team" was just me. I later realized that my insistence on doing everything myself and my reluctance to ask for help led to taking something away from my family. Patterns are difficult to break. After years of living with my teenagers and aging parents, it became a regular thing for them to claim to be incompetent to get out of doing certain household tasks. They knew I wouldn't let them down and would follow through. One such example is that they collectively claimed not to know how to place an order for food, how much to order, or what to order from our favorite restaurants. Regardless of whether I was at the office, an airport, or about to give a speech, I always placed the orders and then texted the information so someone could pick it up if it wasn't being delivered. I am making gradual efforts to remedy this and enlighten my family.

While I enjoy cooking and making family meals, when I arrive home from work late, I usually disregard my children's request for me to pick up takeout. Instead, I reheat leftovers or pull something out of the freezer and into the air fryer or pressure cooker. I've explained that I don't always have time to figure out what they want, place the order and pick it up. I've suggested that if they learn how to place an order, that will solve the problem. They've chosen to learn. While I usually make meals or prepare something for them to put in the oven or microwave when I'm away, I've learned to let go of needing to put a home-cooked meal on the table every evening.

Despite enjoying caring for my husband, children and extended family, I needed to feel that there was more balance and less control of my time. That I had choices and a voice. That I could rely on my husband the same way he relied on me. Now, as I juggle the responsibilities of being a single parent with teenagers and caring for my elderly parents, I have similar struggles. While I love doing things for my family, I am slowly teaching my children that a family is a team that shares the burdens and rewards of managing a household and everyone must do their part to avoid overburdening anyone.

It has been a struggle to transition children into young adults who will succeed independently. I find myself consistently reminding them that shirking their household chores, no matter how big or small the tasks are, sends the message that I work for them and that we are not a team. Often, they respond with: "I don't know how" or "I didn't have time" or "I didn't understand."

I stress that it's also their responsibility to ask questions, learn, and follow through because it is not fair for me to bear the brunt of being solely responsible for day-to-day activities. If they want to honestly engage, they need to be informed, ask questions, and follow through; otherwise, they will continue to be blissfully ignorant and have an unacceptable hold on my time. Bit by bit, they are discovering the benefits of working together. The shift has been slow, but there's less fighting and prodding, and more cohesion and time to do activities together. I'm less worn out and they are happier with more independence, less arguing, and the free time I now have to spend with them having fun. All relationships require effort, but collaborating instead of avoiding tasks or feigning incompetence and ignorance is rewarding and worth the investment.

CHAPTER SEVEN

Imposter Syndrome, Honesty & Humility

"Am I confident in who I am and all I've accomplished, or do I undermine myself and stand in my own way?"

Imposter syndrome is the persistent belief that one's success is undeserved or wasn't legitimately achieved. It's a sense of inadequacy, despite evidence of success and competence. It persists in the form of nagging self-doubt that creates the sense of being a fraud, both intellectually and in your skilled proficiencies. People of all ages, backgrounds, and genders experience this psychological phenomenon. Studies have shown that 70 percent of the population experiences imposter syndrome, with executive women accounting for 75 percent of that group. This perception prevents you from enjoying everything you've worked hard for.

Impostor syndrome can cause real damage by inducing anxiety, preventing self-appreciation, and throwing roadblocks in your path. Despite deserving greater recognition, these sentiments can chip away at your sense of worth. It shows up, not just in your career, but in relationships, other friendships, and in your community activities. It might start in one area, but before long, it can infiltrate your whole life. And when that happens, it robs you of the joy and fulfillment you're entitled to.

Imposter syndrome can be mistaken for discrimination, but analyzing your experiences and feelings can help draw out the distinction. Your own internal beliefs can trigger imposter syndrome, which may lead to feelings of inadequacy. Discrimination occurs when people intentionally or unintentionally engage in behaviors or actions that result in the exclusion or differential treatment of others. It's an *external* problem, while imposter syndrome is an *internal* problem.

The self-doubt that results from imposter syndrome can shake your confidence so much that it casts doubt on your abilities and goals despite your prior conviction of feeling competent. Anyone can fall victim to suffering from imposter syndrome, which is not deemed a mental illness; however, it may take a trained therapist to help you overcome the feeling of insecurity. Through therapy, you can achieve the fulfilling, positive life you deserve instead of one plagued by negative self-fulfilling prophecies and a failure to recognize your self-worth and full potential.

Imposter syndrome is not about your environment; rather, it's about what's going on in your own head. This isn't something being forced on you from the outside. It stems from a distorted self-perception that makes you feel inadequate, despite your achievements. The key is to stop blaming your circumstances and start believing in yourself. Reclaim your self-worth, trust your abilities, and don't let those doubts hold you back.

It's a problem when you consistently fail to recognize opportunities to showcase your accomplishments, potential, and ideas for future engagement and growth. It's a problem when you consistently tell yourself that your worth doesn't rise to the level of others. It's a problem when you hyper-focus on your weaknesses and diminish your strengths, achievements, choices, life experiences, and education.

Certain characteristics define whether you suffer from impostor syndrome. These can include self-doubt, undervaluing your work and contributions, refusing to accept success, and attributing your achievements to external factors. This can lead to setting unrealistic goals, worrying about not living up to your potential, and burning yourself out by pushing too hard.

Part of overcoming imposter syndrome is the ability to recognize when you achieve each of your goals and by owning your accomplishments. It can be a tough challenge if you still doubt your abilities and your right to feel proud and joyful about your success. The difficulty lies in shifting your mindset to actually accepting and taking pride in your success, rather than continuing to dismiss or minimize it because of lingering self-doubt.

In the face of a challenge, anxiety often leads to overcompensating behaviors like working excessively hard, over-preparing, staying up late, memorizing extensively, and rehearsing endlessly. This intense effort can ultimately backfire because after all this preparation, the result may be that you regret even trying in the first place.

Others may not recognize the internal symptoms since you're more inclined to hide your struggles than showcase the extra work you put in or express your negativity. When imposter syndrome sets in, it interferes with the pursuit of realistic goals and the formation of meaningful and positive relationships, which often leads to further regret, deeper self-doubt, and increased negative self-talk. Despite all the evidence that supports your achievements, your core beliefs about your inadequacies don't change. Sometimes your success is credited to others, seen as mere luck, or perceived as falling short and not having the ability to go the distance.

According to Dr. Valerie Young, an internationally recognized expert of imposter syndrome and cofounder of the Imposter Syndrome Institute, the phenomenon can be broken down into five types:

The *perfectionist* sets extremely high standards and believes that, unless they perform a task perfectly, they are flawed and therefore cannot own their achievement.

The *expert* feels like a fraud if they don't know everything about a topic in their field. They are always seeking more information and validation.

The *natural genius* doesn't feel inherently intelligent or competent, but they expect to achieve everything effortlessly. They become devastated by anything less than swift mastery.

The *soloist* prefers to solve and accomplish everything independently, as they consider asking for help a sign of weakness, resulting in feelings of shame.

The *superhuman* believes they should be able to effortlessly juggle multiple roles and excel in each one. They must work harder, faster, and more efficiently, and if they fall short in any role, they feel the burden of shame.

It is possible to overcome imposter syndrome. Dr. Valerie Young suggests reframing your thinking from having an imposter *life* to simply having an imposter *moment*. This small but significant shift in perspective can make it easier to manage and overcome the self-doubt associated with imposter syndrome. Acknowledging that these feelings of fraudulence are transient, rather than a fixed flaw, allows you to understand and address them more effectively.

To determine whether you suffer from imposter syndrome, ask yourself the following questions. Write down both the questions and your answers, then note any situations that come to mind. This can help you understand whether you are standing in your own way, or if there's another factor at play. You can also use this exercise as a tool for discussion with someone you trust, such as your mentor, a family member, your partner, a trained therapist, or a social worker.

- Has imposter syndrome affected my relationships, employment opportunities, or growth?
- What, if anything, could I have said or done differently to achieve a better outcome?
- Do I often compare myself to others and find fault with myself?
- Do I procrastinate because I feel incapable or unworthy?
- Do I expect to always perform perfectly?
- Do I often feel like I am not enough?
- Do I constantly feel that I'm not deserving and don't measure up?
- Do I often feel like I'm not achieving enough?
- Do I often feel that I don't accomplish or learn fast enough?
- Do I often feel inadequate or inefficient?
- Do I often feel that I need to be someone who is better than me?
- Do I often feel undeserving of what I get or incapable of accomplishing what's expected of me?
- Do I compare my actions and words against others and then determine that I fall short?

- Am I dependent on feedback and prone to discount my own feelings where my performance or other accomplishments are concerned?
- Do I feel unworthy of praise?
- Do I feel unworthy of success?
- Do I struggle to believe or accept praise?
- Do I fixate on minor mistakes?
- Do I focus on mistakes rather than accomplishments?
- Do I attribute praise I deserve to others?
- Do I tell others I am worth less than what they think I am?
- Do I judge myself more harshly than I do others?
- Do I diminish or discount the positive feedback I receive?
- Do I unilaterally decide that I am failing, falling behind, or not measuring up?
- Do I lead with uncertainty rather than confidence?
- Do I feel embarrassed to ask questions because I think I'm the only one who doesn't know the answers?
- Do I question what I know to be true?
- Do I tell myself others are smarter than I am?
- Must I criticize myself to find motivation for self-improvement?
- Does my inner critic cause me to work harder than everyone else?

- Is my behavior driven by the fear of inadequacy rather than the excitement?
- Can I accomplish what I need to do without fear of being exposed as a fraud?
- Do I worry that others see me as the flawed individual I see in myself?
- Do I often tell myself and others that I'm incapable of taking on new tasks, employment, or adventures?
- Can I own my failures and call them teachable moments?
- Do I stay stuck in place because I worry about moving outside of my comfort zone?
- Do I worry about not having all the answers?
- Does my lack of confidence prevent me from speaking up?
- Do I worry about the time it takes me to learn or accomplish tasks and reach goals?
- Do I have a longer list of weaknesses than strengths?
- Am I comfortable saying, "I don't know?"

Some questions are purposefully repetitive with the goal of stimulating critical thinking and self-analysis to help determine if you need help finding your value and owning your achievements. There's no such thing as absolute perfectionism, so if you constantly strive for an impossible standard, you'll only end up diminishing your worth and frustrating positive emotional growth and self-esteem.

Plenty of resources are available to help you confront imposter syndrome. If you struggle with it, reach out to a trained professional. With proper therapy, you can tackle your struggles and find out if you're the one limiting your potential.

Keeping a journal can be helpful, regardless of whether you seek therapy or to plan to make changes on your own. Validating and tracking your progress will provide clarity and guide you toward a solution. Making a list of your goals, accomplishments, abilities, training, and experiences is a solid start in assessing your abilities and whether you are truly capable or a fraud.

Journaling can also help you set new goals while staying focused on current ones. Putting thoughts into writing can be daunting because it requires an honest evaluation of what you've done—or haven't done!

Asking for help is a sign of strength and success, not of inability or failure. If you're not into journaling, confide in someone you trust and ask for their feedback on how they perceive you. It's worthwhile to collect feedback from a few people who know and support you, because their similar comments will help you assess the validity of your self-beliefs. Don't just rely on the feedback of one person. It is important to collect feedback from a variety of people you trust to ensure diverse aspects and reliability. This feedback can also help change your negativity into positivity. Record the feedback in your journal and compare it to your list to see if there are similarities or differences.

The feeling of being an imposter occurs when you credit your success to others, luck, or fear of not being enough. When you worry that others will perceive you as "inadequate," that fear controls you, holds you back, and obscures your success. Your accomplishments become overshadowed when they deserve to stand out.

When you own up to being an imperfect human who occasionally needs help, your honesty and vulnerability build trust better than if you try to project an image of always being the best and always being right. The result of honesty and humility is usually a positive, enduring resolution that everyone involved takes ownership of.

Nurturing others while revealing your fears and flaws fosters respect and adds credibility and respect to relationships, even if you aren't ready to fully acknowledge your own success. Use conversation starters like, "I'm not sure where we're going or how we're going to get there, so I want to discuss options with you." "I don't have the expertise required to find the best resolution, but with our combined experiences, input, and resources, I think we'll reach a positive decision." "I'm not sure, but let me put this idea out there for discussion."

These exchanges not only promote humility and humanity, but also establish the groundwork for team cohesion and conquering imposter syndrome. Healthy dialogue allows you to be inclusive and lets others know you value them. Icy relationships often melt and turn into strong bonds when you move forward as a teammate rather than as a lone leader plagued by self-doubt and internal criticism.

Never apologize for being right. Never apologize for asking questions. Never apologize for asking for the things you want. Never explain why you want or need something. Never apologize for having an opinion. Never explain why someone should value you, your opinion, what you want or need, or anything else you do. You don't owe anyone an explanation or an apology for being you. You are enough. You are allowed to live your life in a way that brings you happiness and allows you to soar (unless you're committing crimes or doing immoral acts).

Asking questions holds power, and the product of an inquisitive mind can make profound changes not just for the person posing questions, but for countless others. Nevertheless, there are always individuals who perceive those who raise their hand or prolong a meeting as troublemakers, wasting everyone's time. This is especially true for young women, but applies to women of all ages. Don't assume that asking questions shows vulnerability or a lack of knowledge. When you ask questions, you are demonstrating leadership skills because it shows that you care enough to understand everything, properly connect ideas, and make the right decisions.

Asking questions is a strength that demonstrates your ability to continue learning, strive for excellence, and partner with others who share your goals. Opting to keep quiet out of fear that others will be mad, or your questions will make you look incompetent, is a weakness. It's an assumption that everyone else knows everything and gets everything right, but in reality, it's often the opposite. It's those who question, discuss, and properly connect information who change the world for the better and expose or clarify mistakes and wrongdoing.

For over forty years, I have had the honor of teaching and mentoring thousands of people at different points in their educational and professional paths. The statement I consistently address before answering a question is the preceding apology. The conversation often goes like this:

Me: "Are there any questions?"

Raised Hand: "I'm sorry, I have a question." Or, more often: "I'm sorry, I have *another* question." Hand down. Shoulders slumped. Eyes on floor.

My response, whether in front of a group or an individual: "Thank you for asking. Please, never apologize for asking a question. I'm here to answer them. We can all learn from questions, and if you have one, it's likely some else is wondering the same thing, but isn't brave enough to ask."

Asking questions is a form of owning and keeping your power. It demonstrates a pursuit of excellence, a genuine interest in the subject, and a commitment to doing things correctly. By asking questions, we can promote positive discussions and ensure that all issues are fully explored. Our strength is derived from the exchange of questions and answers.

Adelle graduated high school, college, and law school at the top of her class. Throughout her education, she had been heavily involved with extra-curricular activities and took pride in her ability to handle and achieve more than others. She was always the first to raise her hand in class or volunteer her time. Her excellence in the legal profession led her to become a highly esteemed attorney and eventually a judge. Adelle was the recipient of several scholarly awards and became known for winning unwinnable cases and changing both procedures and laws. She met Evan when they were on opposite sides of a case she won, and they began dating.

Adelle was extremely focused on her career. She set financial goals and surpassed them. She set career goals and achieved them. Although she had no interest in having her own children, as she doubted that she could dedicate enough time to them, she eventually married Evan, who already had children.

Her humble nature and willingness to share credit for her accomplishments earned her an exceptional reputation. Adelle often said she just got lucky and rarely accepted compliments for her hard work and unique style.

Regardless of her achievements and accolades, she always felt behind, inadequate, and unprepared. Her constant worry was that she would be caught publicly without knowing the right answer to a question. Despite understanding that no attorney wins every case, every case she lost sent her spiraling downward.

When Adelle became a judge and some of her rulings were called into question by high-powered lawyers or her decisions were reversed by the higher courts, she became depressed, despite having earned a stellar reputation. Adelle responded to all issues properly but internalized adverse questions and appellate reversals by spending time in solitude, researching and revamping protocols and procedures, and scripting the information in her rulings that she made in writing and on the record. To cope with burnout and feeling incompetent, Adelle turned to alcohol, which became a problem.

Eventually, her withdrawal caught some attention, and she was referred to the Lawyers and Judges Assistance Program. I was assigned to mentor her. We met nearly every week for two years. Aside from working on her sobriety, attending counseling, submitting to random drug and alcohol testing, and attending Alcoholics Anonymous, we worked on her backstory.

Her parents had set such grand expectations, she feared failure and wanted to surpass expectations in every endeavor because that's what she believed her parents and siblings did. Her goal was to surpass her siblings rather than be overshadowed by them.

Despite facing a few setbacks, Adelle worked hard, relearned, and finally accepted that even near-perfect individuals, herself and her family included, had flaws because no human is perfect. She made a list of the things she was doing and cut it in half, keeping only what she enjoyed. To work on positive reinforcement, she began journaling, attending yoga, and setting aside time for self-care every day. She committed at least an hour a day to do the things she enjoyed, like reading, swimming, and taking cooking classes.

Over time, she learned to look at failure and success differently, realizing that by moving forward and doing her best, she was enough. She learned to accept compliments with a smile and a simple thank-you. She stopped bringing her briefcase home and cleared her bedroom of all work-related books and materials.

Her marriage grew stronger, her work performance improved, her sleep quality increased, and she developed new friendships. To her surprise, Adelle learned that her parents and siblings had been worried about her. They never expected her to be perfect; they just wanted her to be happy and find joy in her life.

Adelle realized she hadn't been happy for a long time. She quickly grasped that perfection meant doing her best, not overachieving. She no longer feels like a fraud and says that, for the first time in her life, she feels like an honest, fully connected human. With the help she received, the need to numb herself with alcohol was no longer necessary. She recently received her ten-year sobriety coin.

It's perfectly valid to feel like a fraud, unworthy of your achievements, or inadequate when compared to others; however, those feelings need to be tamed and contextualized before they become so internalized that they cause physical, emotional, and social issues that seriously affect your life. Make it a priority to believe in yourself and take pride in your accomplishments, both personally and professionally, every day.

Luck didn't get you where you are. You created your own "luck" through hard work, persistence, belief in yourself, and the ability to seize opportunities. If you find that this is difficult to accept, find someone to talk to who can help you before imposter syndrome becomes a serious problem.

CHAPTER EIGHT

Integrity & Leadership

*"Are you an inspiring, innovative leader
or a compromised, frustrated follower?"*

Integrity plays a significant role in shaping relationships, yet the consequences of having it or lacking it are often overlooked. It's a powerful character trait that threatens those who lack integrity and who aim to control or manipulate others. Integrity fosters respect, empowers rather than diminishes people, and acknowledges the value of everyone's voice and contribution.

When leaders prioritize integrity, it cultivates trust, honesty, and clear communication, which encourages them to honor and fulfill promises. A leader with integrity is accountable, takes ethical actions, and accepts responsibility, regardless of the difficulty or inconvenience of the tasks. Integrity fosters inclusive relationships by being transparent, promoting open communication, and providing opportunities for immediate feedback.

The foundation of a lifetime filled with fruitful and respectful interactions lies in maintaining integrity in every relationship, which includes being dependable and trustworthy so that strong bonds are developed. It's equally important to match words and actions, along with fostering open communication for both positive and negative feedback, analysis, and decision-making. Integrity is the cornerstone that shapes character, guides choices, and supports decision-making, ultimately cultivating healthy relationships built on trust, reliability, and honesty.

Integrity is a vital quality that encourages and allows necessary conversations about positive and negative issues to occur on a regular basis. The fear of revealing embarrassing information, negative experiences, or uncomfortable topics, as well as the concern of coming across as offensive or harsh, can make certain conversations difficult. Having both easy and tough conversations is essential, because both reinforce honesty and integrity with the common goal of building a mutual understanding, even amidst opposing viewpoints. The goal isn't to "win" but rather to earn and maintain mutual respect.

Shutting down communication, acting out of character, and breaking trust will quickly erode the relationships you've built. It will also raise doubts about your past integrity and cast suspicion on your truthfulness.

Those who lack integrity are often disrespectful. While they bully and intimidate others to prevent them from questioning them, their actions and words contradict ethical and moral principles. They're not only dishonest, but they often use gaslighting, grooming and ghosting techniques to weaken others and enhance their own power. Their unreliability and inconsistency, coupled with their demand for unearned respect, is often evident.

Being in a personal or professional relationship with someone who lacks integrity can have significant psychological effects, such as stress, anxiety, nervousness, sleeplessness, and low self-esteem. In this situation, the key is to shift the blame where it belongs instead of taking it out on yourself. When evaluating a relationship, there are several indicators that suggest a deficit in integrity, honesty, and accountability. Some examples are blame shifting, ongoing dishonesty, unreliability, moral contradiction, and disregarding positive actions.

A law school student, Emily, was on probation after being arrested for operating a motor vehicle under the influence. I became her mentor through the Lawyers and Judges Assistance Program through the State Bar of Michigan. Emily struggled to realize she had been drinking to excess and had become addicted to alcohol. She began treatment, which included individual and group therapy, attended Alcoholics Anonymous, and focused on her education. To validate her progress, it was mandatory for us to meet at least once a month. To become eligible to take the Bar Examination and become a licensed practicing attorney, she needed to overcome her addiction before it overcame her. We met weekly because she was quite certain she couldn't stop drinking on her own and understood she needed validation and support from someone who wouldn't be easy on her and where truth and honesty would be a priority.

Emily had just broken up with her boyfriend, whom she'd been dating since her senior high school year. They attended law school together, where she discovered he'd been cheating on her with another law student. When she confronted him initially, he told her she was crazy. Eventually, she confronted their female classmate, who confirmed the relationship.

Emily skipped class, returned to their apartment, and packed up his things. When he returned, she demanded he leave. He left, but not without hurling a barrage of insults, criticizing how cold, ugly, and overweight she was. He moved in with the girl he'd been seeing behind Emily's back and, shortly thereafter, they were engaged and married.

To cope with her pain, instead of eating, Emily drank. She changed her hair color and style, bought new make-up, tossed out every piece of clothing that reminded her of him, and bought new clothes. When she wasn't studying, she spent time with girlfriends from school who didn't associate with her ex's fiancée. The problem was that her new friends liked to go to the bar after evening classes to drink and dance.

Emily drank right along with them, but instead of dancing, she would drink more. Things got out of control until one evening, when she wasn't feeling well, she decided to not wait for her friends, left the bar, and was pulled over by law enforcement. They arrested her for drunk driving. After being released on bond, she reported the arrest, as law students are obligated to do.

Once Emily finished recounting her story, she tearfully acknowledged that she wasn't making excuses. She was fully aware of the unwise choice she had made and was thankful that she could plea to an ordinance violation because she previously had no prior records and was willing to participate in the Assistance Program.

Emily felt like a fool for trusting her ex and for making an even bigger mistake by drinking to excess. As the tears fell, I handed Emily a tissue and thanked her for trusting me with her story and allowing me to mentor her. I also applauded her honesty and integrity. She narrowed her eyes, shook her head, and said she didn't understand, to which I replied:

"You had the guts to end a relationship that lost its integrity, honesty, and mutual benefits. After he broke your trust, you chose yourself and the good morals you want and deserve in a relationship. You made a tough but enormously powerful choice because you value and trust yourself. That means you're stronger than you think and would rather stay true to your core values. When faced with a tough choice, you put your wellbeing ahead of what you initially wanted in the relationship. You stayed true to your morals and prioritized yourself, choosing an honest, respectful, and monogamous relationship that aligned with your long-term goals for the benefit of everyone involved."

"I thought I loved him, and we were building a life together. I no longer trust myself," Emily said.

"Someone who loves you wouldn't tell you hurtful lies or hide what they were doing. When confronted, they would tell the truth instead of gaslighting you," I said. "I know you feel detached from what you believed was true, but staying with him would have been emotionally demoralizing and would have caused significant damage over time."

Emily continued to see me and followed through on all her treatment requirements. She got stronger every week. However, a couple of months later, she called me from a bar. She was with her friends and had ordered a soda instead of alcohol, but her friends were ordering her drinks. She felt compelled to join them and conflicted between doing what she knew she needed to do and what they wanted her to do.

"Think about this," I began. "They want you to take part in their destructive behavior so they can feel better about themselves and what they're doing. By doing the right thing—not drinking alcohol and returning to your apartment to study—your choices and your leadership will stand above their choices. They want to bring you down. Invite them to rise up and not ask you to drink when they know you can't, and leave with or without them. Watch what happens."

"I never thought about it like that. Thanks," she said and hung up.

When we met the next week, Emily told me she'd thought a lot about our conversations, especially that phone call. That night, she left the bar and only one of her friends left with her. She began looking at people's motives and realized that most of them wanted to bring her down to their level when she wanted to do the right things. Emily stopped trusting those people and stuck to her integrity. It made her feel a lot lighter and filled her with a sense of hope for her future.

When someone encourages you to have another drink, drive faster, stay in a cheating or violent relationship, what they really want is for you to join in their "bad" behavior. This helps them feel better about themselves since you are also now doing it, too. You become an unwilling coconspirator to their immoral behavior, which goes against your values. Their actions strip you of your integrity, choice, and power; however, the power shifts back to you when you walk away.

Sometimes being a leader calls for having difficult conversations without placing blame or passing judgment. I held a supervisory position, which is where I met Sadie, a hard-working young woman with beautifully thick, long, dark hair. She found her hair's weight and heat irritating and asked her stylist for a haircut. When Sadie arrived at work with her new style, everyone fawned over the change; however, behind her back, they gossiped and laughed at how unflattering and outdated the style was. The gossip spread quicker than the E. coli virus, and a "contest" arose to see who could give her the best compliment. When I found out, this did not sit well with me at all. During the lunch hour, I complimented Sadie on her bravery for cutting her beautiful locks to try a fresh style. Within the first day, she already felt better without her heavy mane and figured that, once she learned to style her shorter hair, she would likely maintain it.

I listened, smiled, and nodded. When she finished talking, I agreed that the new length and style would require a learning curve for drying, styling, and finding the right hair products. She agreed. I then said: "Honestly, I think a different short hair style would suit you better. This one looks like a '50s hair style, and it doesn't fit your vibrance."

Sadie ran her fingers through her hair and grabbed a mirror from her purse to look at herself. "I can see your point. Thank you."

The next morning, Sadie bounced into my office sporting a new, youthful haircut that flattered her long neck and high cheekbones. "I want to thank you for your honesty. I thought about what you said and then stared in the mirror for a while before calling my stylist to book an immediate appointment. I wasn't sure what I wanted, but I told the hairdresser what you said, and she showed me pictures of different styles. I showed her which ones I liked and told her to surprise me."

"She did a wonderful job. I'm proud of you for taking a second chance. I'm not sure I would be that brave," I said.

"You're brave and honest. You were the only one who told me the truth," she said and then paused. "I know everyone was making fun of me, except you."

Earning the respect of one person amongst a plethora of others speaks volumes about your integrity. It means you use your power for good, instead of conforming to the negativity that erodes confidence and challenges honesty and integrity. Gossiping reflects a selfish desire to elevate oneself by degrading someone else, which has the opposite effect. It demonstrates a lack of integrity and a compromised sense of morality.

One of my students, Liza, put herself through college by waiting tables and preparing carry-out orders. During her shifts, she earned more tips than any other server, which created some discord. Despite advising management and human resources about the problems, she was left to deal with it on her own. She faced her coworkers, who claimed she stole money or lied about the origin of the tips. They tried to gaslight her to believe that she was wrong and they were right.

Liza held onto her truth, integrity, and power. She started logging every time the manager retaliated by cutting Liza's regular hours, without reason, or ridiculed her in front of other employees. Despite everything that happened, nothing could shake Liza's commitment to her integrity, morality, and honesty.

She liked her job, and she was good at it. The location and hours were convenient for her classes and the other activities she enjoyed. Despite being bullied and working in a toxic environment, Liza refused to quit. She feared both losing her job and confronting her manager, but she was even more scared of the consequences of not standing up for herself.

Liza was determined to quit on her own terms and would not let anyone force her to leave. In an email to restaurant headquarters and human resources, Liza asked for an after-hours meeting with the managers and staff to discuss the issues before she filed formal complaints. Management promptly scheduled the meeting they had previously declined.

At the meeting, the manager said she had noticed discrepancies in the division of tips, which violated the tip-sharing policy. The assistant managers stayed quiet but nodded along with everything she said. The manager declined to raise any of the other issues Liza had brought forward.

Liza looked around the room. With all eyes on her, she sensed that her coworkers knew what had been happening, but were all too afraid to speak up. She thanked the manager for finally calling a meeting and actually listening to her concerns. Liza echoed that everyone did an excellent job and deserved to be tipped according to the policy. Working with the public was difficult enough, and they would only have a positive workplace if they partnered together.

She pointed out that customers never questioned her orders because she always double-checked her work. Patrons often commented that she was the only takeout person they wanted to deal with because they knew she would fill their orders properly. They trusted her to call and ask questions if something wasn't clear or if there was a need for a substitution. Liza's coworkers backed her up and said they appreciated her, yet the manager remained silent.

Liza finished by reminding everyone that, when she took time off, management often asked her to come in because there were a lot of complaints and revenue was down. Again, all managers remained silent, but her team members echoed what she said. Liza's bravery encouraged them to speak out and voice their own concerns.

Others said they were going through the same thing and just wanted to be treated fairly. They wanted a schedule that management didn't use as punishment and a fair division of tips. Liza ended by asking for regular meetings to foster ongoing communication.

The manager claimed ignorance and said that if anything was wrong with tip division, it was an honest mistake. She added that scheduling was organized for the good of the restaurant and based on the requests of all staff.

Everyone makes mistakes. Everyone acts out of character once in a while. However, when behavior contradicts policies and morals, it suggests a conscious disregard for integrity that involves gaslighting, grooming, and dishonesty. When the restaurant staff called her out, the manager became aggressive. She didn't take responsibility for any problems and failed to offer solutions or seek input from the assistant managers.

Upon hearing about the issues that arose at the meeting, the corporation replaced the manager. The new manager is providing Liza and her teammates with an accurate distribution of tips, and Liza has since received three raises and a promotion. She became the assistant manager of carry-out and can attend college and take vacations without worrying about being called in. By fearlessly advocating for herself and her coworkers, she motivated others to voice their concerns instead of succumbing to intimidation and bullying.

CHAPTER NINE

Embrace Change with Voice & Choice

"When change happens, can you adapt, express yourself, and make choices that enrich your life, or does it stunt your growth?"

Change often happens when you least expect it. And when you know it's coming, can you honestly say you've always been prepared for it? People sometimes struggle to embrace change because they're most comfortable with what they already know. Throughout life, everyone experiences change, both good and bad. It's best to embrace change as an indicator of good things to come, more meaningful relationships, and enlightening experiences.

You often have little or no control over change. By taking the time to learn about what needs to change and exercising patience while adapting, you gain control over its impact. When you don't dedicate time to adjust, negative consequences like insecurity, vulnerability, despair, stress, and similar effects take hold.

The way you use change matters, as it can either enrich your life or trigger depression and anxiety. Openness to change increases your chances of success in personal and professional aspects and bolsters your relationship with yourself because changes won't seem so overwhelming. Instead, those changes will yield to your inner power and strength. This is important, as making the right choices during change allows you to conquer the situation and discover valuable insights about yourself.

Change may be uncomfortable, but it pushes you out of your comfort zone, which is vital to unlocking hidden skills, strengths, and stamina, which is crucial for personal growth and development. Like any other skill, the more often you embrace change, the better you become at handling it.

Maintaining a positive mindset and using motivational mantras are key strategies for strengthening your psyche when confronting change. Create your own inspiring mantras and repeat them daily. Share them with anyone else going through the same change as you. Post them on a mirror, door, computer, or anywhere you'll see it regularly. They don't have to be long and convoluted. They can be simple:

I will figure this out.
I will overcome my fear and conquer this change.
I am stronger than I realized.
I will move forward until I succeed.
Failure is the road to teachable moments and success.
There is no time limit to adapting to this change.

I am strong enough to ask for help.
I can help others by setting an example.
My confidence will override my uncertainty.
Change makes me resilient.
Embracing change promotes positivity.
Tackling change with positivity validates my abilities and conquers my fears.
I effectively handle change by refusing to limit myself.

Some changes *might* happen, such as switching jobs, moving, or having a baby. Some are *inevitable*, like the death of a loved one, the end of a contractual obligation, or a child leaving home. Others are only *possible*, like a tornado, recurrence of cancer, or not having the means to repay a debt. When you know it's coming, it's helpful to prepare ahead of time, rather than simply living in denial or avoiding the inevitable. By being better prepared for change, you have more control and can use your voice to better navigate, organize, and formulate viable solutions.

Preparation also alleviates stress, anxiety, helplessness, and fear for yourself and others, while also minimizing disruptions, facilitating smoother transitions, and creating effective plans. While it's impossible to plan for everything, some of these strategies may be helpful:

- create a checklist
- research viable options
- rearrange finances

- organize bills, income, and employment options
- discuss who the changes will affect
- reframe a potentially negative experience into a positive one
- make a list of resources for immediate and long-term needs
- create routines you can stick to or adjust when necessary

These strategies aren't all-encompassing but can help you think about what planning and preparation might be feasible to protect your overall well-being when change happens. Preparation is part of taking control, using your voice, and ensuring that you have choices. Using your voice empowers you to be the author of your own destiny.

Life happens. The choices you make when you initiate change are just as important as the ones you make when changes are forced upon you. By championing change, you take control of your life and experience greater satisfaction and enjoyment. It welcomes positivity, growth, and new challenges that open doors to opportunities beyond your imagination.

Despite the inevitability of change, there will always be people who refuse to accept it and would rather wallow in the past, stay wrapped up in their grief, or let fear hinder their personal growth. It's important to recognize that everyone, yourself included, must accept and honor change in their own time and in their own way. When faced with change, establish the boundaries you want others to adhere to and be considerate of others' boundaries if they're unwilling to adjust at the same pace as you.

Using your voice to implement change is an empowerment that leads to a range of positive outcomes, such as more control over your environment, better decision-making, collaboration, growth, team building, partnerships, and improved quality of life. When you use your voice, you're expressing thoughts and feelings through words. Choose them with conviction, ownership, and a firm belief in what you're saying. Clearly advocate for or against change. Explaining your concerns and feelings is necessary to move forward in a positive direction.

Your truth, needs, opinions, and visions might not align with societal norms, but don't let that discourage you from expressing yourself. Speaking your truth is powerful, but you must consider the tone of your voice. When you raise your voice in anger, you lose your power and credibility. Therefore, before speaking, take time to consider your desired outcome and your audience. Listen and be open to meaningful discussion.

Whether it's advocating for yourself, someone else, your community, your nation, or the world, you have the choice to speak up and make a difference. One of the best ways to effectuate change is to use your voice, even if it causes dissention. When dissension is met with open and honest discussion, it can pave the way for positive outcomes and change.

These discussions don't imply that the dissenting voice or the voice for change was the *right* one. It means that through collaborative discussion, active listening, and respectful partnership, you can establish a well-reasoned outcome that will serve as a catalyst for meaningful change. Take charge of the changes coming your way by being proactive. That way, you keep it together and maintain a healthy mindset, even when the worst happens.

By considering both the troubling and the advantageous aspects of change, it's possible to reframe the narrative and turn negatives into positives. Remember, just because you consider a change to be a good thing doesn't mean someone else won't think it's a bad thing. Change isn't a one-size-fits-all situation. If you asked for it, educate others so they understand why you want to implement a change. If you didn't instigate or recommend the change, explain why it's necessary. Even if they don't like it, understanding why change is necessary minimizes conflict, anxiety, and fear.

Once the change is in effect, determine which actions proved to be most useful so you can apply them in similar situations in the future. From there, create a framework to evaluate change with the flexibility to alter the course if the previous change didn't go as expected. By analyzing and being open to modifications to your framework, you can build or rebuild confidence and overcome challenges that push you out of your comfort zone.

Anne was a free spirit who pursued a career as a photographer. Despite having college degrees in technology, psychology, and education, she always listened to her inner voice and gravitated toward her creative side when considering employment opportunities. She gave up pursuing more degrees, fearing she would become a lifelong college student.

Although she had no trouble finding employment based on her degrees, she always quit to pursue her passion for photography. She loved reaching out to public figures and offering to photograph them. Anne garnered an impressive portfolio, but at age thirty, her mother passed away. She packed up her apartment and moved back home to care for her ailing father. Shortly thereafter, the COVID-19 pandemic struck, and she couldn't travel or take photographs, except when she took walks to get some exercise.

Over time, her stress level began spiraling out of control. Anne's father became so ill that she couldn't leave him alone. She had food, prescriptions, and other necessities delivered, and could only leave the house to attend her father's medical appointments. Money was running low, and she feared that if she hired help, they would be forced to sell the house or file for bankruptcy.

Out of desperation, Anne reached out to Veterans Affairs and then to hospice for comfort care assistance. Both agencies provided some relief, but the journey ahead was fraught with many obstacles. Her father preferred that she care for him, and he gave other caregivers a tough time unless she was there to supervise. Anne never imagined that her father, who had always been a healthy, larger-than-life man, would become dependent on her. The mental and emotional stress caused such a drastic change in lifestyle that she suffered weight loss, migraine headaches, sleeplessness, and depression. Some days, she found it difficult to leave her bed.

Occasionally, she responded to text messages or phone calls from her friends. During a Zoom call, I spotted deep circles under Anne's eyes and unprecedented fatigue. She described the drastic changes in her life and expressed her struggle to cope. Our conversation covered living without regret, valuing family, and speaking up when we need help. She promised to find a therapist and to do something positive for herself every day, even if it was just saying something nice to herself in a mirror.

When we discussed the choices Anne had, I reminded her that she was the only one standing in the way of using her creative talents. To take care of her father, Anne needed to take care of herself and make good choices that made sense for each of them, which included using her voice to advocate for what they needed. We worked together for a few weeks, talking about options, prioritizing her goals, and assigning small tasks that she agreed to accomplish each day.

Her first job was to find a therapist. That was easily accomplished after she got a referral from her physician. The next task was to alleviate her financial issues. She created a website and began selling her photography. Next, she began painting, crocheting, and doing needlepoint. Anne posted some of her creations online, which led to expanding her art, taking orders, and teaching virtual lessons. Shortly after the pandemic ended, her father moved into a nursing home. The onset of severe dementia made it unsafe to keep him at home.

Today, Anne is physically and mentally better than she's ever been. Her therapist aided in the diagnosis of attention-deficit/hyperactivity disorder (ADHD). She maintains regular appointments with her therapist, has taken up yoga, and takes her prescribed medication, which not only calms her but allows her to focus. She feels healthy in every way.

Anne decided to prioritize her self-care and overall happiness by continuing her work in the creative field. Her online store is thriving, she visits her father daily, and she's overcome her fear of change. While she knows her father won't live forever, she's confident that she will adapt to the change and continue living a joyful life after his passing.

From a very young age, Connor realized he was more interested in being with boys. He was extremely outgoing and had an equal number of male and female friends. His female friends often preferred to confide in him rather than their female friends because he was nonjudgmental and had an aptitude for giving good advice. He enjoyed attending school activities and functions with a group of friends rather than dating one person.

During his junior year of high school, his mother urged him to ask one of the girls he often spent time with on a date. To avoid his mother's constant mantra about dating a nice girl and his father's disapproval, Connor asked Tina to prom. No one knew Connor was dating Phil, who attended a neighboring high school.

Tina knew Connor was gay, so she went along with the scheme. Phil invited Tim, a friend of his whom Tina knew and liked. Phil would then be Connor's date. Both Tina's and Connor's parents took at-home prom photos, and then they switched dates. Neither couple believed their parents would discover their deception. And they didn't until the yearbooks came out. Pictures made both sets of parents question what was going on. Tina didn't want to "out" Connor, but he saw it as an opportunity to speak his truth and change his life.

Prepared for the worst, he packed a suitcase with essentials and put it in the trunk of his car. After dinner, Connor asked his family to stay seated at the kitchen table because he needed to tell them something important. His mother asked if it was about college. Connor took a deep breath, released it, and sat on his shaking hands. "I like men. I like girls as friends, but I won't be dating or marrying any of them."

His older brother said, "I knew it."

His younger brother shrugged and didn't say a word.

His sister said, "It figures."

None of his siblings gave him a hard time or seemed to care that he was gay. They asked to be excused and left the kitchen. His mother cried, lamenting that she'd never see him get married or give her grandchildren. She made the issue about her.

His father blinked stoically, then stood up from the table and started pacing. After a brief silence, Connor felt a sense of relief and said: "I'm sorry if I've made you unhappy or uncomfortable, but I figure it's time for you to know who I truly am."

His father finally spoke. "We don't understand this, but all we've ever wanted is for you to be happy and live your life." His mother nodded but remained tearfully silent after that.

Connor continued to date Phil, but they no longer hid it. They became roommates in college, and after several months, Connor's mother began inviting Phil to family functions. She has come to accept the relationship and respects her son's right to make his own choices.

Connor is finding joy in having honest relationships with his family and those he includes in his life. He is grateful for the people who stood by his side and extends his best wishes to those who don't understand him and cut him out of their lives.

Connor continues to use his voice and to stay true to himself and those he cares about. With a focus on child psychology, he aims to continue his college and career journey by empowering others to find their voice.

CHAPTER TEN

Language Matters. Listen, Think, Speak.

"Do I use open-ended questions that encourage honest answers, or do my word choices create intimidation, silence, or assign blame?"

Language is a fundamental part of human connection that has the power to uplift or tear people down. Your first few words convey positivity, negativity, trust, confidence, or deceit. When coupled with action, language becomes a powerful force. Every interaction has the potential to make an impact or create confusion and miscommunication.

People often take their language choices for granted if they serve their purpose. Nonetheless, it's important to clearly express your intentions. Be mindful of how you communicate, as your words and tone can shape how others perceive you. The consequences of using the wrong words or gestures can have unintended, long-lasting effects that include misperceptions by both the recipient and the speaker of the information. The wrong statement, even when unintentional, can ruminate on the recipient's mind for many years to come. If you're not careful, you could lose the opportunity to get the information you need, and the recipient may put shields up for future conversations because they're now expecting the worst outcome instead of the best. In fact, even when you think they are listening, they may not be hearing any new conversations because the previous upsetting one overtakes their ability to concentrate and shift gears.

To be a successful leader, you must possess strong communication skills and be an exceptional communicator. Practice active listening and employ appropriate language to cultivate personal and interpersonal growth through effective and respectful communication. Your communication skills and language usage can either enhance or detract from your presence in a room or in conversation.

The best-case scenario involves establishing trust and practicing active listening, which allows you to make informed decisions and take action. Leaders gain both trust and followers by mastering communication skills.

The vernacular we use, whether at work or in personal relationships, should not marginalize us or anyone we communicate with. Language is a powerful tool that allows us to communicate a wide range of thoughts, from abstract concepts to concrete ideas. It facilitates problem-solving, the exchange of knowledge, and the expression of philosophy, creativity, and other types of messages. Effective communication requires using verbal and nonverbal language to share information without stifling or impeding responses.

Choosing the right words can determine whether you receive an honest response, a biased and unbelievable response, or no response at all. It also has a significant impact on your future relationship with the other person. The way you choose your words and present your thoughts is crucial. Through questions and accompanying gestures, you convey your assumptions, which can either build trust, sow distrust, encourage openness, or foster polarization. Language brings us together or drives us apart.

When deciding what to say, consider the implications of each word. Reflect on the underlying meaning and how your words may be interpreted in different ways. This may seem like more of a language lesson, but the manner in which you communicate information is key to your credibility, sincerity, and ability to find the information you want. If you don't care about the information, then don't bother asking for it. If you care, then let your actions show it. Your good name, reputation, and trustworthiness will shape how the rest of the world sees and interacts with you.

To be effective, use age-appropriate language and avoid business jargon unless you are with others of a similar background. This doesn't mean talking down to someone, but it does mean using language your audience will understand and relate to. Choose words that encourage open dialogue and mutual respect, rather than appearing interrogative or controlling.

Language has the power to transform, create opportunities for greater understanding, enhance cognitive skills, improve decision-making, spark curiosity, and drive meaningful change. The wrong language can stifle a conversation, steer it in the wrong direction, or lead to bias, discrimination, and exclusivity. Choosing the right words in a conversation can spark essential change by challenging preconceived notions and improving any situation.

It is important to analyze questions and other statements that elicit a response that will result in the ability to properly interpret the answer's meaning, context, and potential bias. Sentence structure and word choice can have a powerful influence on a person's thoughts, responses, and feelings. Poorly worded questions may cause the listener to misunderstand what you're asking or avoid answering you all together.

When you ask open-ended questions beginning with "what, when, where, how, and who," it shows that you are attentive, compassionate, and eager to hear the answers. It is best to avoid *why* questions as they inherently shame and blame. *Why* questions should be limited to research and science. Let me share an example of an interaction I had with my youngest son where I had to explain the harsh reality of using why questions.

One morning when my twins woke up to watch cartoons, they started fighting over a blanket. My son came rushing into my room, tears streaming down his face, complaining that his sister had taken the blanket from the couch. My response: "Instead of fighting, why don't you just get another one out of the closet?"

His response: "Mom, you're blaming me!"

I immediately apologized, grabbed another blanket, and settled him in. I realized what I should have said is: "How can I help?" The *why* associated blame, triggered his anger, and shut him down.

When delivering my motivational speeches, I convey this message and my feelings about the usage of *why*, and present various alternatives to consider. A middle-aged woman approached me, explaining that she and her college-age daughter had a fantastically close relationship and spoke daily. While she asked a lot of *why* questions and received a lot of information, it wasn't great information. I challenged her to drop the *why* in favor of using other terms, promising that it would lead to better conversations with her daughter and elicit more specific information. She tried it for a few weeks and then emailed me, saying that, to her astonishment, I was right. She now uses *why* sparingly, if at all.

Before engaging in conversation, it's worth exploring the abundance of simple word choices that can lead to more meaningful conversations. When you choose the most appropriate words to align with your objectives, you showcase leadership qualities, empathy, and respect for the people you communicate with. With the right words, you stay well-informed, cultivate heightened awareness and sensitivity, and enable everyone to make improved decisions with the most suitable options.

When speaking for an extended period, such as during a lecture or when answering questions, it's important to vary your words and tone to keep your audience engaged and responsive. Be cautious and make an effort to steer clear of angry, hateful, prejudicial, racist, sexist, misogynistic, presumptuous, offensive, or threatening words, as they can incite violence, negativity, and even riots.

Treat the words you use like valuable investments, just as you would with money. Be careful, wise, frugal, and show kindness, regardless of how tense the situation is. Before engaging in a meaningful conversation, you must carefully select the language you'll use, taking into account the person, group, context, and desired outcome. Language can change the course of a conversation, your relationship with the receiver, and the outcome. If you want the best result, invest in using the best language.

Don't offer apologies for someone's hardships, such as losing a loved one or surviving a violent assault. Saying you're sorry transfers the burden back to the person who then replies: "Oh, it's okay." In that way, they are "healing" you, so *you* don't feel badly about what happened to them. The aftermath of this conversation leaves them with an increased burden to bear. Instead, consider altering your response to open-ended statements or questions in a way that demonstrates your genuine concern, attentiveness, and willingness to help. Some responses you may consider are: *How are you doing? Is there anything I can help you with? Would it help to talk about it? I am there for you if you need anything, even just someone to listen o*r sit with you.

Word choices become the framework of conversations, dictating whether they create a sense of connection, adversity, or polarization. With the rise in communication through artificial intelligence, texting, and email, the connectivity between people through language is often compromised, which can result in unintended outcomes. Just because you champion good causes and invite honest, well-meaning discussions doesn't mean you're always right. Through open, positive communication and a focus on empathy and understanding, you can promote diversity and inclusion and inspire cohesion and growth. This will have a rippling effect that will reach everyone you engage with, because that is the power of language.

Attitude also matters. Life has ups and downs, and often the language you use mirrors your mood. If you're in a mood, take a few seconds to pause and make a thoughtful choice. Choose to say, "Yes, and . . ." which is positive and upbeat, instead of, "Yes, but...". For example, when you return from vacation, and someone asks: "Did you have a nice time?" Consider the tone of each response and notice the differences. "Yes, *but* we had terrible connections, and the weather was lousy," or "Yes, *and* we met some lovely people and the food was fantastic."

I recently came up with a solution to a problem by creating a user-friendly, timesaving form. A colleague's response was very off-putting and insulting. When I gave her the form for input, she looked it over and said, "How did *you* think of this?"

I replied, "Because I focus on solutions, not complaints." Her comment, coupled with her tone, was condescending. She could've said any number of things like: "Nice work," "Great idea," "This is a good solution," or simply, "Thank you. I'll look it over and get back to you." Any of those would have been preferable to insinuating that I wasn't smart enough to have thought of such a helpful solution.

When relationships turn bad or conversations don't go well, consider the words used and the difference between what was meant and what was understood. Try to structure the next conversation differently. Compare responses. Don't feel obligated to pre-plan your conversation, rather, make small word-choice adjustments to convey your desire for meaningful dialogue. When conversing with multiple people, try to be inclusive rather than exclusive, as this will result in better relationships and more positive conclusions.

Think about some of the word choices below and how they impact you and others when used. Also, consider which word or phrase is more welcoming, powerful, and meaningful.

"THE" VERSUS "A"

The is a definite term you use when offering advice or solutions. *A* offers a variety of choices, not the best answer or solution. Evaluate the situation by looking at it in reverse, from end to beginning. Determine what your intended message and outcome are before deciding which word to use. When you are clear, your message is stronger. Using *the* instead of *a* is clearer and defines an answer.

Consider these statements:

"The solution is . . ." (clear and definite)

"A solution is . . ." (one of many choices)

"The problem is . . ." (clear and definite)

"A problem is . . ." (there are many problems)

"The supreme sandwich . . ." (clear)

"A supreme sandwich . . ." (could be any available)

"IF" VERSUS "WHEN"

Use *when* instead of *if* because *if* has a negative connotation and *when* emphasizes positive reinforcement. While this isn't true in every instance, think about the context before making your statement.

Consider these statements:

"If you do *x*, *y* will happen (negative).

"When you do x, y will happen (positive).

"WANT" VERSUS "NEED"

Change *want* into *need* when asking for something definite and immediate. Use *want* for a desire and *need* for a necessity. If it's important, be clear. Both you and the recipient will be much happier. Using the terms properly is empowering because you'll get what you're really asking for and find contentment with yourself and those around you.

Consider these statements:

"I want new shoes." (implies sometime)

"I need new shoes." (implies now)

"WHAT" VERSUS "HOW"

Changing *what* into *how* can transform negative thinking and inaction into positive thinking and action. Both words can build stronger connections and be transformational, motivational, and useful for problem solving and critical thinking, but consider the impact of each separately. *What* can be interpreted as asking someone to explain or justify themselves because *what* suggests they did something wrong. *What* limits the ability to fully explore a situation and receive critical information. *How* asks for information, explores the situation, and opens a dialogue, which fosters meaningful discussion.

Consider these ***What*** questions with a hint of blame versus the ***How*** questions asking for information:

"What did you do?"
"How did that happen?"

"What caused you to make that decision?"
"How did you make that decision?"

"What made you think you could do that?"
"How did you decide to proceed?"

"What reasons do you have for your actions?"
"How did you determine the next step?"

"I" VERSUS "YOU"

When giving advice or compliments, change *I* into *you* to evoke the sincere compliment you intend to give the recipient. Using *you* instead of *I* can be construed, in its barest form, to mean that you're taking credit away from the person you meant to praise. By avoiding phrases such as "I think" or "I am," you keep the focus on the recipient instead of yourself. Give the recipient the spotlight they deserve. Otherwise, while you are giving a compliment, you're also taking credit for "thinking" that what the other person did was amazing. Unless you share credit, ensure the other person receives full recognition. You'll have even more respect for each other.

Say the following sentences out loud. Contemplate how each one makes you feel and decide which phrase sounds more powerful, authentic, and encouraging.

VERSUS

They receive full credit:	**You take some credit:**
"You're fantastic!"	"I think you're fantastic."
"You did the work."	"I'm proud of you for doing the work."
"You're awesome!"	"I think you're incredibly talented."
"You're a gift to the world."	"I think you are a gift to the world."
"You deserved the promotion."	"I thought you deserved the promotion."
"You continue to achieve great things."	"I see you continue to achieve great things."
"You're the best of show."	"I believe you're the best of show."
"You earned this."	"I watched you climb the ladder of success."

Why should be reserved for scientific inquiries. *Why* is a complete sentence that asks the recipient to explain their actions. When someone is in distress, ask open-ended questions that don't begin with *why* to find out how you can help. Unless you've taken the time to think about whether it's appropriate, avoid *why* questions to elicit helpful and honest answers. Consider some of these questions:

VERSUS

Shames and Blames	**Tells recipient you are open to their answer**
"Why are you late?"	**"How are you?"**
"Why didn't you do your homework?"	**"When is your assignment due?"**
"Why are you wearing that?"	**"Where are you going?"**
"Why didn't you tell me?"	**"What would you like me to know?"**
"Why are you going alone?"	**"Who's going with you?"**
"Why are you acting like that?"	**"How can I help?"**

When you're truly engaged, you can pick up on what's not being said and address it. You don't have to change the world, but you can change the trajectory of another person's world. Language matters so much that it can save a life, change the course of history, or be the lifeline someone needs.

CHAPTER ELEVEN

Be The Insider In Your Life

"Do you feel a sense of worth or like you don't belong?"

The human experience is all about connection, but feeling like an outsider is something many can relate to. Most children go through this feeling at different points in their childhood, but it often continues into their adult years. The sense of belonging isn't an all-or-nothing situation. Everyone fits in somewhere, but no one fits in everywhere.

As you navigate life, it's crucial to recognize your feelings and their triggers, especially when you feel like an outsider or less than perfect. If you're someone who easily adapts or strives for perfection, you may feel like an outsider because conforming to and pursuing perfection can hinder your ability to be authentic. When you can't adapt or achieve perfection, you feel disconnected from everyone, including yourself. When you don't learn to appreciate and embrace your positive attributes, you lose valuable parts of yourself and become consumed by negativity.

A lot of situations can create a sense of being an outsider, where you feel like you don't belong or are different. Starting over at a new job or school... disclosing your sexual identity... having greater or significantly less wealth or socioeconomic status... having numerous educational degrees or none... celebrating different religious beliefs... coming to terms with having mental or physical issues... abusing substances like illegal drugs or abusing alcohol... dressing differently... or having unusual hobbies. Deviating from societal expectations can create discomfort and a feeling of not fitting in.

When society labels you as "unusual," change your perspective and rewrite the narrative. Rather than focusing on the misconception that being an outsider is a flaw, embrace your uniqueness as an outsider because that's where your value lies. Your original thinking is a manifestation of your unique individuality.

Being different or feeling like an outsider can be advantageous, as it sets you apart as a leader rather than a follower. Your individuality is a gift, not a liability. By daring to be different, you become a powerful force in challenging followers, making you an innovative thinker and a changemaker. Becoming the leader of change doesn't mean you're always right or always wrong, but rather that you make decisions based on relevant and correct information. An outsider is someone who fearlessly raises important concerns and chooses a different direction from those who conform to societal norms or accept the status quo.

If you can't change your perspective and see that being an outsider is a positive thing, it's time to reflect on what makes you feel this way. That might mean seeking help from a trained therapist or other mental health professional. I developed a series of questions and answers to help shift your negative perspective into a positive one. Gaining insight into the reasons behind your feelings is always helpful.

To begin, write down instances where you felt like an outsider, including who was with you, where you were, the time of day, what triggered the feeling, and how you reacted. This will help you explore, understand, and discuss your feelings. It will also help you identify patterns that may help you shift your perspective.

As you do this, remember that your feelings are valid. Embrace and own your uniqueness. Establish boundaries and make your own rules instead of following others. You have the right to surround yourself with people who see, hear, appreciate, and respect who you truly are. No matter what anyone says, you deserve to feel safe, be happy, take charge of your life, and forge a positive path to your destiny.

Consider these questions to help you reflect on the experience of not fitting in. Use the answers provided or come up with your own.

Q: Do I spend my personal time with supportive, like-minded people who see the real me?

A: Yes. I'll join groups and attend social or educational functions that are important to me. I choose to work, form friendships, and take part in activities with people who truly honor my feelings.

Q: Are my colleagues and the company I work for supportive and like-minded?

A: Yes. I seek meaningful employment that makes the difference I want in my life, my community, and the world.

Q: Who is constantly critical of me, even when I'm at my best?

A: I set boundaries and expect people to honor them. I will remove the negative and critical people in my life. I choose to be around positive people who appreciate my uniqueness and want to have discussions that lead to positive and meaningful outcomes.

Q: Am I open to new opportunities to connect with like-minded people at work and in my personal life?

A: Yes. I will take the time I need to develop meaningful relationships.

Q: Do I feel disconnected from some people but not others? Who are they and what role do they have in my life?

A: I will seek relationships where I feel connected and respected. I will not give anyone power over me. I will only welcome individuals into my life who genuinely admire and appreciate me without passing judgment.

Q: Do I feel bored with life or in need of change because fitting in makes me miserable and anxious?

A: I understand that life is full of possibilities, and by embracing change, I can receive extraordinary gifts that will enrich my life beyond imagination. I'm not afraid to change course because my intuition and common sense will lead me to where I'm meant to be.

Q: Do I think of myself as a perfectionist?

A: I understand and own that I am imperfectly perfect and make mistakes, just like everyone else. Perfection is impossible, so I embrace imperfections in myself and others.

Q: Am I frequently adapting to others, yet not being honest about myself and my desires?

A: I embrace my true self and will not discount myself by adapting to others. Instead, I will seek people who appreciate, embrace, and respect me as I am.

Q: Is the culture of the area I live or work in a poor fit for me?

A: I can change where I live or work and go to a place where people see the world the way I do, think and dress like I do, and agree that diversity, equity, and inclusion are important.

Q: Do I feel unsafe, unheard, unloved, or disrespected in the presence of certain people, groups, or situations?

A: I have the right to say no and distance myself from anyone or any group where I feel marginalized, unsafe, or disrespected. I will seek people I'm comfortable with.

Q: Do I feel like everyone else fits in, and yet I'm the only one on the outside looking in?

A: I acknowledge that the world is a large place, and not everyone thinks, acts, likes, owns or wears the same things. Embracing my uniqueness enhances my happiness, doesn't limit me, and fosters harmony in my relationships. I am unique, therefore I experience the world in my own unique way. My unique perspectives enable me to achieve my goals and dreams, and live an exceptional life.

Q: When I speak up about issues I care about or express my needs, do I feel alone, ostracized, or like I don't fit in?

A: I choose not to remain silent, change my opinions, accept that my needs won't be met, or compromise my worth. I will seek people, activities, and employment where I am heard and appreciated.

Q: Am I prone to feeling oversensitive around people who think differently than me?

A: I choose to appreciate my unique perspectives and way of thinking. Some people think I'm a troublemaker, an overthinker, or that I'm simply wrong, but I embrace our differences. I accept their opinions and demand that they accept mine. When someone disrespects me, I keep my power and integrity, and walk away or set boundaries. I acknowledge that those who think outside the box, including myself, are instrumental in making the world a better place.

Q: Do I keep to myself because I feel like I don't fit in?

A: I enjoy spending time alone. My time is valuable, and I choose to spend it with people who respect and admire our similar and unique qualities. I will selectively cultivate mutually beneficial relationships.

Q: Do I become overwhelmed when I'm around those who think differently?

A: My unique skills, talents, and perspectives make me an asset. I appreciate others who think differently and embrace our differences. Talking about our differences creates solutions and broadens my worldview.

Q: Am I afraid to speak up when I have a different opinion than those around me?

A: No. I value being a nonconformist, individual thinker, and I expect everyone to respect my opinions and perspective, even when they're different, because I respect the opinions of others. My unique experiences, opinions, or worldview will not diminish my worth.

Q: Do I look for differences rather than similarities in others?
A: I will not assume that I don't fit in with people who have different opinions or disagree with mine. Supportive, like-minded people don't have to agree on everything. I will determine whether mutual respect exists before deciding the appropriateness of the relationship.

Q: Do I feel like I must follow popular trends to fit in, and if I don't, does it make me feel like an outsider?
A: Popular trends and opinions don't influence me. I focus on what's important to me and enhances my life, regardless of what others think is important or interesting.

Q: Do I often feel that the well-worn path I've been on causes me to lose my way rather than find it?
A: I'm comfortable paving a new path, despite the challenges it brings, because I'm in control of my life. I embrace the path that makes me happy, even when others go a different way.

This is not an all-encompassing questionnaire, as there are infinite situations and factors that influence your worldview and how you fit in. The world is a better, more interesting, and bountiful place because everyone is different. If embracing your uniqueness doesn't bring you solace, consider exploring options that can help you cultivate a positive mindset. Think of these questions and answers as a starting point to reflect on situations that caused you to feel unworthy or like an outsider. Flipping the negative script to a positive one will remind you of your worth, normalcy, and the importance of your voice and feelings.

The questions and answers are designed to help you normalize your feelings and reduce the anxiety of feeling inferior. If you have difficulty fitting in, suffer from anxiety or depression, or simply can't seem to fit in, please seek professional help. Complete this questionnaire and take your answers to your therapist to initiate a meaningful discussion. Sometimes it's as simple as having an opening line and the rest of the discussion flows naturally.

The fear lies in avoiding the discussion, not in having it. Letting fear and pressure control you keeps you feeling like an outsider. Stay in control. Speak until you are heard, and know that you fit in perfectly, just as you are!

When I was a high school senior, the legal drinking age was eighteen. My friends and I were responsible and made sure we had a designated driver to take us home after a night out. There wasn't much to do on weekends, so we often went to one of two bars that had terrific live bands. I have fond memories of those evenings we spent together, dancing and laughing.

After several weeks of doing the same thing (sporting event one night and dancing the next), I started suggesting other options. My brother and I had joined a bowling league during my junior year and his sophomore year of high school. I found the sport relaxing and enjoyable. Since none of my close friends were in the league, I suggested we switch things up and go bowling. I also expressed my distaste for drinking, and I had quickly learned that alcohol and my body chemistry didn't mix well.

They shrugged off my idea *and* assigned me the designated driver role. I justified their decision because I enjoyed dancing sober and meeting people from other high schools, so I had no qualms about being the perpetual DD. Nevertheless, I persistently suggested going bowling or playing cards. *Anything* else, really, but they continued to shrug off my suggestions.

Despite having a good relationship with my group of friends, I began feeling like an outsider. One evening, when I was feeling particularly frustrated with the same old routine, I announced that I couldn't drive because I had reserved a bowling lane. My friends laughed and told me they'd see me at school. I went to the bowling alley, and at the end of my second game, I looked up and my four best girlfriends were there, bowling shoes in hand.

From then on, we changed things up. From a broader perspective, this was a small matter, but for a teenager, it was a major issue. It's interesting how even the tiniest thing that sets you apart can make you feel like an outsider. I reminded myself that I choose how I want to spend my time. Trusting my gut and choosing to be the director of my own life has always allowed me to be the insider, not the outsider.

I relayed my bowling experience to my twins when they couldn't decide what they wanted to do for their fourteenth birthday. While I allowed each of them to make a choice and celebrate with friends separately, I hoped they would also consider having a joint event. I suggested bowling. They laughed and told me they would never suggest such a geeky activity to their friends. They wanted to do the same things their friends did.

The disagreements went on until it was nearly too late to invite anyone. I brought up bowling again, even if it would just be the three of us. My daughter reluctantly agreed and invited two friends. Not wanting to be left out, my son also invited two of his friends. They warned me that if anyone made fun of them, it would be all my fault.

After five games of bowling, they admitted to having so much fun they asked when they could go again. I suggested they join the high school league and offered to invite the parents so I could bowl, too. Surprisingly, all six teenagers agreed. They even found the prospect of watching their parents bowl rather amusing.

My children instantly went from feeling like uncomfortable geeky outsiders to insiders who knew how to have fun. While they didn't immediately join the league, I remained hopeful that they would, eventually. The transition from being an outsider to an insider takes time. Every small step matters. Every choice matters. You matter.

Lacy was in her late twenties when she lost her mother to a brain aneurysm. A year later, she lost her younger brother to a blood disorder, and six months after that, her father passed away from heart failure. Her multiple losses caused her to suffer from depression, anxiety, anorexia, and suicidal thoughts. Lacy felt like an outsider because she wanted to be with her family and struggled to deal with their absence. She was inconsolable and lost her joy for living. She spent hours sitting with her cats and going through pictures and other memorabilia, praying she would soon be reunited with her family.

Every birthday, holiday, or other significant family event worsened her downward spiral. No one she knew could relate to her pain. Despite initially showing sympathy, as months went by, people began commenting on her inability to move on and suggesting ways for her to recover. People told her how she should feel, what she should do, and how she should cope.

She couldn't return to work and eventually spent more time in the hospital than at home. Lacy's medical team included a psychiatrist, a psychologist, and a social worker. They repeatedly placed her on suicide watch and kept her on a variety of medications to help her cope. After a few years of more downs than ups, she learned to trust her medical team and her therapist.

In time, Lacy rebuilt her life and became gainfully employed. She made a few friends at work and a few high school friends reached out to her. As much as she tried to spend time with them, she found it difficult because none of them could relate to her pain. She attended extended-family functions and the occasional work event but spent most of her time alone.

Lacy's unique experiences shaped her worldview, which set her apart from others. While others had lost loved ones, no one in her circle had lost every immediate family member. Being the sole survivor at such a young age was daunting and made Lacy feel like an outsider who didn't deserve to live a happy life.

Lacy discovered a way to bond with her young niece, who had always looked up to her. She was present at her birth and saw her regularly as she was growing up. Their close bond was the reason her suicide attempts failed. And when her niece was nine, she made a point of regularly calling or texting Lacy to invite her to family, school, and social events.

Ultimately, she realized her niece was the one who motivated her, but Lacy needed to be the hero in her own story. She attended everything her niece invited her to, including soccer and volleyball. During practices and games, she immersed herself in the game and deepened their bond.

Her niece's parents and other family members were skeptical of her prolonged grief. Her extended family members commented about getting over her losses, dealing with her weight, and changing her demeanor. She was often ordered, rather than asked, to attend their family events, which she declined unless her niece was going to be there. Despite being surrounded by her extended family, Lacy felt like an outsider because they were consistently critical and didn't truly listen to her.

When Lacy decided to get out of the rut she was in, she switched up her routine, which began with taking her niece to parks to practice soccer and volleyball. She treated her to ice cream, movies, bowling, rollerblading, and manicures where they chose the same nail polish color. Lacy made sure they had plenty of quality time together, just the two of them.

Spending time with her niece was initially the only thing that gave Lacy joy and made her want to live. Their connection gave her a sense of purpose. For nearly a year, she was her sole lifeline. It took nearly three years, but she eventually broadened her horizons and learned not to internalize the opinions, beliefs, and demands of others.

Lacy kept photos and other mementos of her parents and brother in a special place in her apartment and began adding pictures of the fun times with her niece. She began traveling, parasailing, skydiving, and taking long hikes, always keeping her father's camera in her hiking bag. She photographed her adventures and posted the beauty she captured on social media.

Once people started sending Lacy the watercolors, sketches, and oil paintings inspired by her photographs, she felt a genuine connection and appreciation. The people who enjoyed her photography and whom she met on her travels became her people. She finally felt like she belonged.

A lot of Lacy's pictures featured rainbows, flowers, and butterflies, which were symbolic of the things she enjoyed with her parents and brother. She began to believe that her family was with her, just in a different form. The more support she got from like-minded people and her niece, the more she felt like she belonged, and she eventually let go of feeling like an outsider.

Lacy is now living a productive and bountiful life. Instead of relying on medication and seeking escapism to destress, she finds solace in photography and deepening her relationship with her niece. She has begun dating and continues to widen her circle. To enhance her well-being, she embraces meditation and mindfulness, and fosters close bonds with compassionate, trustworthy friends and coworkers.

The worst environment for feeling like an outsider can be at work, especially for a new hire. Most people with full-time jobs spend as much or more time with their work family than the people they love.

Throughout my bountiful career and various employment changes, my coworkers often treated me like an outsider because I'm a woman. It didn't matter that I was well educated or had lots of experience. When I was new on the job, in every position I've held, I took the time to learn, listen, and observe before I interjected myself and proposed changes.

While starting a new job can be exciting, it can also make you feel like an outsider. And the feeling doesn't just creep in. It hits you in the face. Company procedures are unfamiliar. Inside jokes between coworkers go over your head. No one has earned your trust, nor has anyone earned yours.

It can be overwhelming to know what to say to certain people. When I was elected as a district court judge, I had about twenty years of legal training and had served in the Michigan Army National Guard Judge Advocate General's Corps for eighteen years. I was the first female JAG officer in Michigan's history. In that position, I served as defense, prosecutor, and judge, depending on the situation. In addition to teaching law school, I gained a variety of other experiences that would serve me well throughout my career.

The problem was that I replaced a seasoned judge with three decades of experience. The chief judge retired a few months later, which made me the new chief judge—and the only judge—until the vacancy was filled.

While everyone was respectful, I felt like an outsider because legal training didn't cover inside court paperwork or procedure, so I had to learn it on the job. I knew that, regardless of what the clerks did, the paper trail had to follow the law and the orders of the court. Despite decades of immersion in law, I was consistently told, "that's not the way we do things," or "we've always done it this way."

Frustration quickly set in, and I began questioning myself. Conforming to what they had been doing was wrong and unsettling. Fortunately, I had a wonderful court administrator whose job it was to help me run the courthouse. I pulled together the court rules, statutes, and other documents that weren't being implemented correctly and brought them to her. I explained the difference between how things were being done and how they should be done.

During a meeting with the court clerks, I outlined the new procedures that needed immediate implementation, which resulted in a tremendous outcry and threats of revolt. I stood firm and the court administrator backed me up. I made it clear that if the new procedures didn't work, I'd be open to revisiting them.

Much to my delight, the feedback I received was all positive. The new procedures saved everyone a lot of time and reduced their stress. Morale, cohesion, and comradery improved. The staff began including me and asking questions about making other changes. They treated me like one of them, and while it didn't happen overnight, I stopped feeling like an outsider. The key was trusting my gut and opening that line of communication.

CHAPTER TWELVE

Success *For* You

"Is my mindset focused on things happening to me or for me?"

Life happens. It brings good, bad, surprise, disappointment, and everything in between. It's a relentless teacher that helps us understand ourselves and the world. Life is a series of opportunities that make us better, stronger, and more confident, although it doesn't always seem that way when things don't work out as planned.

How do you enjoy a quality life when your plans don't work out? How do you erase thoughts like: *Why me? Nothing ever goes my way. Why does everyone else have it so easy?* This battle within normalizes wallowing and allows the cycle to continue. Holding onto that mindset breeds unhappiness and negativity. It undermines confidence and grows like a weed, multiplying with every negative thought.

Despite our best efforts, history repeats itself even when we make conscientious changes. So, we use failure as a chance to learn from experience. After all, we are in control of our lives, right?

Wrong!

The truth is, the universe replicates situations until we accept that we must embrace change, adapt, and allow life's situations to unfold. Everything happens for a reason, and everything happens *for* us, not *to* us. We give up our victim mentality in exchange for a growth mentality. When you relinquish what you think is control over a situation, you'll discover that the outcome may be different, but could ultimately be better.

Gaining insight and realizing that something happened *for* you cultivates confidence and eliminates negativity and stress. That realization allows you to discover new possibilities that you might have otherwise missed. Once you learn to trust that life's teachings always turn into triumph, you'll release the burden of fighting fate. Ultimately, you'll stop trying to control the things you truly have no control over and letting life happen for you, not to you.

It can be difficult to acknowledge that someone's decisions shape their individual history, considering the freedom they have to make choices. While everyone has the right to live as they please, their choices are grounded in a willingness to learn and honor the lessons that result from their decisions, rather than continuing to fight them solely out of closed-minded stubbornness. Life gives us wisdom, and we need to embrace it.

Your past was influenced by your reactions, words, and the way you perceived each situation. By reflecting on the consequences of your past choices, you can live a productive, happy life free from the weight of disappointment and stress caused by unmet expectations. Changing your mindset is an opportunity to reshape your history with positivity and growth.

Take a few moments. Close your eyes. Think back to those troublesome moments you wish you could erase or change even slightly, and how those events rattled you. Maybe you posted a picture or made a comment on social media after having a few drinks, or out of spite. Maybe you said something politically incorrect in the heat of the moment at a public event. Maybe you bullied, taunted, or assaulted someone on impulse. These are all teachable moments that didn't just happen to you, they happened for you.

Consider the list you made of your perceived failures and regrets. How does the way you think about those events affect your future? What separates those who live in happiness and positivity, despite having a long history of hardships, and those who wallow in the despairs of woulda coulda shoulda? The difference is: those who choose happiness over despair understand that things happened for them. Using every hardship as a learning opportunity transforms disappointments into positivity.

Developing this mindset takes time. It wasn't something I intuitively knew, rather it was something I learned out of exasperation. I made a deliberate decision to analyze events in my life. Although I wanted to rewrite history and make different choices that would yield different and better outcomes, I realized that making changes was the key to shaping the history I wished to experience. When I made my rather lengthy list, I scrutinized and evaluated my history. The truth was undeniable: every setback and problem led to better and bigger outcomes. All I needed to do was change my way of thinking. It was clear that my life happened for me, not to me.

I know myself well, and I knew that changing my mindset wouldn't be easy. I used to prefer being in charge and setting a path in stone that avoided problems, provided stability, and delivered all the benefits I expected. Life's truths taught me that charting any course in stone isn't realistic. And it was frustrating. Life always intervened, tossing in the unexpected, and I found myself juggling more than I could handle, falling behind, and then playing catch-up. I had to pause, reflect, and give myself permission to accept that I couldn't control life. After coming to that realization, my strength, happiness, and peacefulness flourished.

Take the time and consider your journey, and not just since you became an adult. Consider your childhood, too. What happened to you? Can you flip the script and see that every event with an unexpected outcome had a lesson for you?

When I graduated from high school, I didn't get a party, a gift, or accolades. My family expected me to do much more, so graduation was just a milestone, not a reason to celebrate. It was, however, a life-changing moment because my father's words have been etched in my brain ever since. After I got home from my high school graduation ceremony, which my father didn't even attend, he said to me: "You've graduated. You're eighteen. What you do in the world now is for you, not for me. You make a mistake, it's yours. If you do something great, it's yours. The decisions you make will shape you, steer your path, and be a part of your story forever."

At eighteen, my still-developing brain barely scratched the meaning of his words. My way of thinking, while appropriate for my age, was superficial. I thought: *Wow, I'm free! I'm an adult and I can do whatever I want.*

Decades later, I understood the meaning of his words. They were the lifelong gift that held me accountable for all my decisions, good and bad. The truth of his words compelled me: I alone would reap the benefits or burdens of my choices, and only I could bail myself out if I failed. Subliminally, it led me to realize that I'm always the hero in my own story, and how I interpret events is vital to my psyche, personal growth, and happiness.

While my father and I have always had a rocky relationship, he taught me that my decisions and experiences happen for me, not to me. This concept served as my analytical guidepost when things didn't go as planned. I came to understand that it's impossible to predict everything, so I had to change my way of thinking and accept that every life event brings both benefits and hardships. I learned not just to reframe disagreeable situations, but to flip them into teachable moments and positivity.

This realization prompted me to further analyze my father's gift: I would always have choices to make. I can either feel victimized, out of control, or powerless, or I can decide to take advantage of the benefits with a winning attitude.

To apply my father's message in your own life, you have to understand a few key principles. When something happens *to* you, you are the target of the action. There's a negative connotation because it suggests you were affected, regardless of the outcome. In contrast, when something happens *for* you, it carries a positive connotation that suggests you influence the actions that stimulate your growth and shape your character. Maintaining this growth mindset is key to maximizing your ability to navigate your life successfully with incredible confidence.

In my role as a general trial division judge, I regularly sentence defendants to jail, prison, or rehabilitative programming either inside prison or outside if they were on probation. I often witness defendants turning their lives around and making good choices rather than succumbing to negative outcomes, excuses, and the feeling that they will never measure up, so why try?

Stanley, accompanied by his attorney, stood before me, ready to be sentenced. He was addicted to methamphetamine, and when he didn't have his drug of choice, he used massive quantities of marijuana and alcohol, or any other drug available, which was often heroin or cocaine. The prosecutor advocated for a prolonged stay in prison. Defense counsel advocated for rehabilitation, followed by long-term probation.

Stanley acknowledged he was an addict and expressed his plan to go home. He promised he would attend rehabilitative programs and comply with all conditions of probation. He needed to work to support his children and help his mother, who had cancer, and his grandmother with early-stage dementia.

I sentenced Stanley to a term of three-years of probation with one-year upfront jail time, which included an immediate transfer to long-term residential substance abuse treatment (no less than ninety days) once a bed was available, and then continued treatment on probation, which included following all recommendations of aftercare. Once he completed residential treatment, the balance of the jail would be held in abeyance and would be used to remind him of the importance of his rehabilitation if he violated the conditions of his probation. If he did poorly during the intense probation I ordered, he would be treated the hard way—significant time in prison followed by five years of parole. I made it clear that if he did well, he could be released from probation early.

I don't have to explain my rationale for sentencing. When the defendants realize that what I'm doing is for them, rather than to them, they can overcome obstacles and make positive changes, because they have a right to be happy.

I had a brief conversation with Stanley, intending to help him recognize the flaws in his thought process and the disconnect between his promises and the choices he made. "You chose to get high, knowing you had children and an ailing mother and grandmother to care for. You can't help your family until you help yourself. Dead people can't help anyone. After you help yourself by getting clean and sober, you can properly tend to your family."

Stanley nodded. "I know you're right."

I proceeded with sentencing and framed my orders with the goal of rehabilitation to heal and benefit him, not just in the moment, but for a lifetime. When I finished, he said, "I accept your decision. I did this to myself."

I leaned forward to truly capture his attention. "You may not like me now, but I'm doing this for you, not to you. You've hit the bottom. Now it is time to rise above," I said, holding his stare. "I believe in you. I know you matter. You need to believe that you matter. Think about the trauma that drove you to check out, push the pain down, and numb yourself. Come back with your children and show me the magnificent things you've accomplished clean and sober. We'll take a picture."

Stanley nodded. "I appreciate you giving me this chance. Nobody has done anything to show they believe in my ability to change and deserve a second chance. Thank you. I'll be back to take that picture." He crossed over the threshold of the courtroom into the holding cell with his head held high and an aura of renewed positivity and confidence.

Stanley completed rehabilitation and was reunited with his family. He's living a clean, sober, productive life, and has since told me how grateful he is for what happened because it prompted him to make positive life changes. He came by my courtroom with his youngest daughter, and we took that picture I'd promised him. It was a very proud moment for him and for me. Now he's passing on his life lessons to others in the support groups he attends.

Not long ago, a friend contacted me in a state of distress after being laid off because his company was downsizing. Despite ten years of loyalty, anger consumed him as he saw the company attacking him and his excellent work. He wanted answers. He wanted to file a lawsuit. He wanted to erase the feeling that he wasn't good enough to be rehired in a different department.

All of this was out of his control. I gently reminded him that he'd mentioned needing more of a challenge at work and had sent an application for a job opening he'd found on LinkedIn. I suggested that he had unintentionally sent a message to the universe, indicating he was ready for a change. And the universe answered.

We talked about going through his out-briefing with a positive attitude so he would get letters of recommendation to help him find a new job. He resisted this approach because he still wanted answers, but I convinced him to stay focused on the contacts, skills, and growth he'd acquired during his time at the company. I helped him make a list of everyone he'd met through his former job, including colleagues and potential job leads. Next, we listed his qualities and the sort of jobs that would feel more like fun than work.

He acknowledged that he'd applied for other jobs while he was still with the company because he wanted new, more challenging employment. The layoff happened for him, not to him. As he applied for work that interested him and spoke to his creative side, he let go of the need for answers. During the ensuing job interviews, he exceeded company expectations and accepted a position that paid nearly twice his previous salary at a company that values his creativity and talent.

Teachable moments arrive when they're supposed to. It's challenging to see events as learning experiences when you constantly believe everything is being done to you. That kind of thinking can lead to self-doubt, depression, and anxiety unless it's turned into positive thinking.

Sometimes the comfort of familiarity can prevent you from venturing out into the unknown where new opportunities await.

This was the case with my middle child, Johanna. In her first year of college, she was happy with her employment, courses, and long-term boyfriend. I assumed that she, like most young adults, would jump at the chance to move out on her own, away from house rules and parental control. I waited. I prompted. I even offered to help. Finally, she found an apartment.

On the day she moved in, the ceiling above the shower caved in. Johanna broke the lease, returned home, and didn't give moving out another thought. She rationalized that the situation with the terrible apartment happened to her because she could only see it online because of the COVID-19 restrictions in place. After that experience, Johanna wasn't eager to move into another place that might fall apart. She promised to move when the time was right. The problem was, the time never seemed right.

As a mother, I want to make sure my children can take care of themselves, make good decisions, and learn from their mistakes. I won't always be around to help them, so kicking them out of the nest and teaching them to "adult" while I can is important to me.

Initially, Johanna wasn't sure she wanted to own a home, but after considering the exorbitant rent prices in the college town and the poor condition of apartments near campus, she finally agreed to look at properties. After months of searching, I bought her a three-bedroom condominium with an attached garage. It was in a safe area and she could afford to maintain it on her own income. She also had friends who would rent from her to help cover the monthly payments.

We closed in early August, and Johanna began packing her things. She moved over a few boxes, and then a few more. Although the property was move-in ready when I bought it, seven months passed before she actually moved in. Johanna made excuses about why it took so long. She had a lot to pack... her cats needed time to get used to the move... she had to find roommates. She wondered why I was doing this to her. Why did I want her out of the house? Why couldn't she leave on her own terms when she was ready?

Johanna's boyfriend moved in, and they immediately got to work organizing their household. I bought a Litter-Robot as a housewarming gift, so the cats had a litter box that was easy to clean and made her life easier. Setting up automatic bank withdrawals for the mortgage payments proved to be a minor problem. Additionally, there was a leaky faucet and some plumbing work that needed attention. Johanna set those issues on my shoulders, all because I "did this to her." She expressed her frustration over not knowing how to deal with these issues and said I needed to fix everything.

I was empathetic, listened, and agreed to help only if she agreed to be on a conference line when I dealt with the issues so she could learn to "adult" and handle whatever homeowner issues arose in the future. She agreed, albeit with reluctance.

By keeping her word, Johanna learned from those teachable moments that she was not only competent, but also capable of handling adult situations. She has since acknowledged that everything that happened laid the groundwork for her future, including life's unexpected surprises. Once she realized it was misplaced, she let go of the blame she'd placed on me and others, and understood that everything happened for her, not to her. Because of this experience, I became the proud mother of a confident daughter who is successfully adulting.

When you think about your life—where you've been and where you're going—think about the outcomes of your decisions. Remember not to beat yourself up. Don't be taken hostage by the woulda coulda shoulda. Instead, banish those accusatory words and embrace the positive lessons. Join me in taking pride and ownership of those teachable moments by realizing that everything that happens *to* you is for you.

CHAPTER THIRTEEN

A Fully Assembled You

"Is the relationship I have with myself healthy?"

Maturity, adulthood, and personal growth don't fully encompass the development required for a productive, happy, and healthy life. The frustrating part for a lot of people is their inability to take the time to understand who they are and who to include in their lives. Everyone needs time to learn; however, maturing is unique to each person and the journey can be influenced by unexpected life events.

I call being mature "fully assembled" because I've taken the time to really analyze myself and list my needs and wants. I set goals and boundaries. There's no one-size-fits-all formula for creating such a list, because everyone is unique. My list has changed as I've grown, and it's also helped the way I see other people. I decide if and how they fit into my life.

To have a healthy relationship with yourself, you must be fully assembled. That doesn't mean being perfect, as there's no such thing. So, how can you be fully assembled when perfection implies being perfectly imperfect?

Being a mature adult isn't just about your age. It's about fully grasping the world, making decisions, and conducting yourself accordingly. True maturity involves self-love, fulfilling your needs, and embracing who you are without apology. It also means having the strength to walk away from toxic relationships. When you cultivate a healthy relationship with yourself, your other relationships can be built on honesty, equality, and lifelong mutual respect.

Everyone has flaws and makes mistakes, including me and you. Recognizing this and accepting it allows you to be real, relatable, and forgiving. People can confront and address their flaws, and if they need help, they have options such as counseling, separation, self-help, and meditation.

When you help others reach their potential without exhibiting jealousy or malice, it's a sign that you're confident and fully assembled in the most important ways. Relationships thrive when people support each other and face problems together. By maintaining this positive connection between yourself and the people you have close relationships with, you can overcome imperfections and ensure that you remain whole, valuable, and worthy.

When you have a healthy relationship with yourself, you can better assess when and how to help others, especially if it involves some personal cost. Some relationships are worth the investment, or cost, while others aren't.

Your ability to make those challenging determinations confidently and without regret or guilt will only come once you're fully assembled.

While it's normal for feelings and relationships to change over time, it's critical that you learn to control any urges to blame others for those changes or demand that they change to fit your expectations. Those actions are futile, negative, counterproductive, and don't change the situation or the dynamics. Consider your role in any upset and evaluate how you contributed, and then work on changes to avoid similar occurrences.

It takes time to develop the maturity to understand the world around you. Maturity comes with age and personal growth. It isn't a race that ends at a finish line, rather, it's a continuum that requires focus, commitment, persistence, and honesty. It involves adopting a goal-oriented mindset and respecting others' lives and goals without passing judgment.

You'll know you're fully assembled when you can truly appreciate who you are, own your failures and successes, speak up when you need to be the voice for yourself or others, collaborate in a spirit of positivity, and make sacrifices for the good of those you care about.

You can't always choose your families or who you work with, but you can choose your friends and partners—the people who have your best interests in mind and promote you, not demote you.

When you're fully assembled, it becomes clear who should be part of your life and it gives you the strength to release toxic people from your life. Many people, including me, advocate for the theory that you must become your own best friend before becoming someone else's, and while that isn't wrong, there are other perspectives that need to be included because they offer clearer insights. Think about your favorite movie and its lead character. Ask yourself if you're the star in the movie of your life. Explore your needs, fears, and who's truly pulling the strings. Understand your feelings, likes, dislikes, goals, and boundaries, and why they matter. Take that leading role and make your needs, goals, and boundaries known. See who deserves a supporting part in your life's story, who simply gets to be a viewer and who doesn't get a role at all.

Putting time into developing the script and your starring role will never be a waste of time. Holding onto negative or draining relationships is counterproductive, but letting them go frees you up to fully embrace who you are and who you're meant to be.

Think about a puzzle with missing or broken pieces. While you may have an idea of what the picture is supposed to look like, it won't be clear or finished until all the pieces are in place. It's the same with building a house. If the foundation is cracked, the house will have problems or eventually crumble. The same goes for human relationships, only they're more complex than houses, because people have feelings, choices, and flaws.

Why the comparison? Because you need to be as well-put-together as possible on the inside as on the outside to attract people who respect and appreciate you just as you are.

Part of this journey is taking the time for exploration, reflection, and decision-making. Often the excuse is: *I'm busy. I'll have to steal some time for myself*, which is nonsensical. You can't "steal" what's yours. You own your life, time, and decisions. Don't "steal" time from yourself, make time for yourself. If someone complains about how you spend your time, rethink that relationship. Consider whether their complaint is valid or if they're trying to control your time for their own benefit.

Instead of saying: *I don't have time for that, but I'll try to fit it in*, say, *I'm choosing not to do that*. No further explanation is necessary. Stop taking a backseat to your own wants and needs and placing others first. You can only truly give to yourself if you have something to give. That means you must own your leading role. Feel whole and be whole before giving away or sharing any part of yourself.

While loved ones may take priority at times, don't lose yourself in their drama and trauma. You are not obligated to let others disassemble you or fix their problems. Remain fully assembled in your starring role, and if others feel entitled to become the director of your movie, it is time to consider walking off the set, so to speak.

I have always enjoyed romance novels and movies. I'm intrigued by real stories about successful relationships, especially those rare couples who are truly partners in a deeply committed marriage or partnership. Despite my desire to embrace and imitate the perfect friendships and romantic relationships portrayed in real life and fiction, I wasn't ready for a marriage proposal at twenty-one.

The contrast between what I know now and what my younger self should have known is far greater than what I could have imagined. What I found out much later was that it simply isn't possible to have a quality, trusting, and developed relationship without being fully assembled. And it's equally important to have a fully assembled partner. When I learned that the human brain isn't fully developed until age twenty-five, I realized I shouldn't have gotten married any younger than that.

I don't have any spare parts to give away, and sharing my life isn't the same as losing parts of myself to someone else. The bottom line is that you can't commit to someone else until you commit to yourself and become your own champion. When you commit to yourself and discover who you are, you will naturally be drawn to people whose values and goals align with yours.

Cultivating lasting connections requires patience over passion. Focus first on building friendship before romantic feelings, compatibility before deep camaraderie, and comfort before commitment.

I met my husband in my senior year of high school. He was two years older than me and lived less than two blocks away. Although we attended different Catholic high schools, we had plenty of mutual friends. We ended up going to different colleges and began dating after he unexpectedly showed up at my college dorm.

He and a few friends were on campus for a football game, and he decided to find me. I thought that was amazing and our relationship immediately flourished. We had similar "old country" family values and future goals. I graduated a year early and got accepted to law school for the following September.

After we got engaged, my fiancé's father suddenly passed away from a heart attack. Instead of going back to college, my fiancé returned home to run his father's business. We were too young and naïve to understand the devastating effect his father's death would have on him, and it should have been a red flag to postpone our wedding. Timing dictated that we should get married between college and law school, or after I graduated from law school and passed the bar examination.

There was nothing special or memorable about our engagement. This should have served as yet another red flag to postpone, but I was focused on my career goals, and he was focused on ensuring his father's business continued to flourish. Neither of us was fully assembled. Instead of learning more about each other, we each focused on separate issues.

My gut told me something wasn't right, but I didn't listen. I left the door open, not knowing that was another red flag. When I found a wedding dress I loved, I tried it on, stood in front of a mirror and my mother, and fainted. Another red flag. We chalked it up to not eating breakfast.

In the church parking lot, my soon-to-be sister-in-law said, "Are you sure you want to do this?" I laughed and proceeded to enter the church.

When the bridal music began, my father held out his arm, just as my mind screamed, "RUN!"

He jokingly said, "It's too late to back out now." We marched toward the altar and my awaiting fiancée. I'd been ill with a severe cold during the days leading up to the wedding, and when it was time to light our unity candle, I didn't have enough breath to blow out the match. The priest asked me if I was reconsidering. I smiled, waved the match, and Dave helped me blow it out. Little did I know that once I said, "I do," he didn't.

I became more invisible with every year of marriage. My husband ignored my needs, instead focusing on his career and leaving me to handle law school, the children and the household. I filed for divorce seven years later after realizing I needed a partnership, not a dictatorship.

He tried to fix the marriage by pouring himself into his work. He'd become a realtor and decided making more money would solve all our problems. I stayed busy, after passing the bar examination, with work, the children, and multiple projects. Eventually, we went to marriage counseling.

The therapist asked us to draw something that depicted how we perceived marriage. Dave drew two circles: a big one representing himself, and a little one inside it to represent me.

I drew two circles like a Venn diagram. The overlapping part represented our marriage, where we made joint decisions and combined our separate experiences. Anything outside the overlapping region was what we decided for ourselves.

The therapist held the pictures up and said, "There's no way to remedy these depictions. This is a discussion the two of you should have had before getting married." After that, my husband immediately stopped attending the counseling sessions. I stayed to learn how to navigate the divorce process and address our children's needs to ensure they understood the divorce was our issue, not theirs.

I can't stress enough how important it is to seek counseling after major life transitions or traumatic events. It may surprise you to find out the information that a complete stranger can pull out of your head. I met Rhonda through a client I represented who was one of Rhonda's patients. Rhonda was a licensed therapist who dealt with addiction. I cross-examined her because she made a recommendation against my client having unsupervised parenting time. As the custody battle unfolded, we eventually learned that neither of us was right, nor wrong. Our clients (the parents) had lied to us, and the truth came out when the children were interviewed by the court.

Rhonda and I became friends after that. We were both single mothers and our children were close in age. At first, I thought Rhonda was quite in tune with herself, her family, and the world. She was personable and kind, and her hair, makeup, and clothing were always flawless and in style. But as I got to know her, I realized her outward appearance camouflaged many imperfections.

Rhonda didn't know herself at all, and her acts of kindness were driven by personal gain. She always worried about what others thought of her, and she went to extraordinary measures to ensure someone else was to blame for her problems, personal and professional.

Rhonda's first husband was a doctor. She blamed their divorce on him for cheating and left him just weeks after the wedding, even though she was pregnant. She got married a second time to a lawyer and walked out on him months after their first child together was born. Again, she blamed her husband's dishonesty as justification for a divorce. A year later she married a broadcast journalist. Six months after her third marriage she filed for divorce, citing that his family was interfering with their relationship.

I knew each of Rhonda's husbands through social and work events long before I'd met her. When her third ex-husband was lamenting on social media and posting that he intended to get her back, I grew concerned and let Rhonda know. She frowned on the use of social media and didn't understand how it worked.

Instead of understanding that I was looking out for her mental and physical health, she screamed at me, claiming I was disloyal because I had social media connections with her exes. "How will it look that my friend is still friends with my exes?" She spent nearly two hours calling every fifteen minutes, screaming the same things.

Unfortunately, after that, I had to block her and end our friendship. I had no choice. I realized that, despite her training and outward appearance, Rhonda was far from being fully assembled. That was the true reason behind the breakdown of her marriages and countless other relationships, including our friendship. Rhonda's anger and insipidness toward things beyond her control revealed her profound dissatisfaction with herself, her lack of understanding about her life and the world around her, and her disconnection from even her most fundamental needs.

Rhonda's next husband was a doctor. His income enabled her to quit her job, and they moved out of state, away from family and friends. She didn't repair any relationships before moving and only reached out to people when she needed something, including me.

What's clear is that Rhonda marries men with graduate degrees, prestigious careers, high income, and an assumption that they will make her happy. Until she digs deep and understands who she is, and what she really needs and wants, she'll continue to leave behind a devastating trail of broken relationships.

Until she's fully assembled, Rhonda will continue blaming others and living in a state of unhappiness and frustration. Her disassembly causes others, even those who are fully assembled, to become or feel disassembled, even if only temporarily.

Although I'm saddened by the loss of what I thought was a good friendship, I made a fully informed, mature decision, and my family and I are better for it. I wish Rhonda all the best, but I am my best without her.

CHAPTER FOURTEEN

Be Your Own Hero

"Am I the victim, villain, or hero in my own life story?"

Heroism is often portrayed or defined as someone who selflessly puts their own life at risk for the greater good of others, but being a hero is so much more than that. Above all else, being your own hero involves honoring yourself, your needs, and your identity. It means intentionally showing up for yourself with kindness, understanding, and compassion.

Heroes inspire hope, help us heal, keep us safe, share wisdom, and serve as role models. To be a hero is to embrace honor by rejecting passivity, acting in defense of others despite fears of negative consequences, and choosing morality over personal benefits. Being a hero is a multifaceted and nuanced concept, as it's completely situational. While heroism includes saving someone from a catastrophe, it's more about supporting yourself without the need for external validation. Validation isn't necessary to take control of your life and make choices that align with your desires and needs.

Unapologetically being the protagonist in your own life story acknowledges that you make yourself a priority. This doesn't mean you don't care about others. In fact, the opposite is true. When you genuinely care about and value yourself, you extend that same value and care to others.

There are some drawbacks to attempting to be a "hero" for others. First, you can inadvertently perpetuate negative behaviors and deny individuals the opportunity for growth and self-discovery. There's a fine line between being a hero and an enabler. Second, being a hero just to flaunt your perfectionism, power, or control is not a commendable act. This type of heroism often leads to negativity, resentment, and anger. Take time to consider your actions and their consequences. Being a hero is a serious responsibility.

To be a hero, you must first contemplate its definition and what heroism means on a personal level. You'll need to know when to push back against external forces and when to address internal struggles. Replacing bad habits with good ones, transforming negativity into positivity, and respecting boundaries are all part of this journey.

Recognizing your strengths and weaknesses allows you to be your own hero during the good times as well as the bad times. Evaluate what influenced your strengths or brought about your weaknesses so you can learn from them, keep to the path of growth, and steer clear of choices that become problematic.

Heroism includes asking for help when you need it and offering help when you can. Strive for higher standards, better results, and excellent treatment. Show concern for your goals and don't settle for less than you deserve. Demonstrate resilience and continue moving forward confidently over freezing in fear. The heart of bravery is showing up for yourself and others and making good choices every day.

Rather than engaging in self-bullying with thoughts like, "I'm so stupid ... I should've known better ... I'm never going to get this right ..." lift yourself up and say, "I'm smart enough to master this ... I learn from my mistakes ... I'll overcome this and try again ... I am resilient ..."

You get the idea. Flip the script and tell yourself something encouraging, motivating, and optimistic. If that feels challenging, consider what advice you'd give a friend, and then treat yourself as that friend.

Anyone can be the hero in their own life story, but you must first acknowledge your commitment to yourself. No more relying on someone else to swoop in and save you. You've got the power to get things done and the responsibility to course-correct when your life veers off track. It means taking accountability for the mistakes you made and being accountable—no more blame-shifting or excuses. Learn from those teachable moments, analyze them, and use that knowledge to keep moving forward.

Opportunities are out there waiting for you, so go seize them!

The opposite of being the hero in your own life story is being the villain. Nothing impedes your progress or stagnates you more than self-sabotage. Sometimes it's difficult to determine whether you're the hero or the villain because outside influences cause you to doubt yourself.

Think about some of these questions. If you answer yes, you aren't being your authentic self. Instead, you're relinquishing your power and playing the role of the villain in your own life.

- Do I make excuses for others' bad behavior?
- Do I tolerate others' negativity, insults, or other terrible acts?
- Do I make excuses for not chasing my dreams and goals?
- Do I stay with people who make me a lesser priority?
- Do I associate with people who hinder my happiness and ability to be myself?
- Do I follow my own agenda or make someone else's a priority?
- Do I wait until others have made their plans before making my own so I don't risk offending or imposing on others?
- Do I offer my time, talent, and gifts to others, seeking approval and validation without expecting or receiving the same in return?

- Do I stop myself from saying what I want or speaking the truth because I fear what others will think?
- Do I change my actions or responses because I fear how others will perceive or treat me?
- Do I allow the opinions of others to influence my sense of self-worth?
- Do I tell myself that someone else's needs are more important than mine?
- Do I prioritize aligning with what others are committed to, rather than staying fully committed to my beliefs and aspirations?
- Do I let people into my life who want to direct me?
- Do I allow people to cross boundaries I've set?

You have the absolute right to keep your power and oust the villain who tries to take it away. Act with conviction and incorporate yourself as the hero into your decisions, life, and persona. This undertaking means you must change your mindset and adjust your attitude. Recognize that you are just as deserving as anyone else when it comes to experiencing joy, love, happiness, goal achievement, gifts, promotions, and anything else you desire. Your aspirations, wants, needs, and opinions matter, and they trump what others demand of you or think about you. Make choices that inspire and empower you to reach your full potential. Release any negative criticism that undermines your true value and identity. Be truthful about who you are, speak authentically, and let go of the need to please others.

Sometimes it takes a tragedy to realize it's time to make that change. Melanie had already been married to Nathan for several years when tragedy struck. She was an interior designer, and he was an architect. They often worked on new building projects together, and when Melanie received compliments for her work, Nathan accused her of flirting.

Nathan used guilt to discourage her from spending time with friends and coworkers, claiming they didn't spend enough time together. He frequently told her no one would ever love her like he did, and that she would make him her priority if she truly loved him back. She started feeling guilty for spending time with other people and began ignoring calls and declining invitations to go out with family and friends.

Without realizing it, Melanie became isolated. She and her three sisters had always been close, and as they became worried about her, the sisters demanded she meet with them to catch up. Melanie agreed and met them for coffee before work, a time she realized Nathan never asked where she was.

Melanie never mentioned meeting her sisters to her husband, but when he couldn't reach her at work, he called her cell phone and accused her of cheating. That morning at the coffee shop, she quickly thought up a lie and said she'd pulled over to have the air in her tires checked. After hanging up, she dropped a few bills on the table and scurried out of the restaurant, telling her sisters that something had come up. After that, she stopped meeting for coffee.

It wasn't long afterward that Nathan began grabbing Melanie by her clothes and pulling her close to him. He'd scream in her face and then toss her aside. His anger toward her escalated to physical violence. Although he never touched her face, the assaults often left handprints and other bruises, and carpet burns when he dragged her.

Nathan checked the mileage on her car, tracked her phone, and strategically placed cameras in their home under the guise of safety. Melanie had to start wearing long sleeves, turtlenecks, and fully buttoned shirts to work. Eventually, she quit her job to take care of Nathan.

When he dragged her up the stairs to their bedroom and she tumbled halfway back down, she fractured her wrist and broke two ribs. Nathan apologized profusely and drove her to the emergency room. On the way, he constantly reminded her of how accident prone she was, and that she'd tripped over her own two feet.

When the doctor wanted to speak with her alone, Melanie confessed that she believed he would one day kill her. The doctor let her use his cell phone and she called her oldest sister. The next call she made was to the police.

The doctor stayed with her until they arrived to arrest him.

Nathan had been in the hallway making a fuss. A nurse brought him back into the room with Melanie and the doctor, and fifteen minutes later, two uniformed police officers made the arrest.

With the support of her family, Melanie testified against Nathan, who was convicted of aggravated domestic violence. A no-contact order was in place and Melanie filed for divorce.

She moved in with her older sister and only spoke to Nathan through her lawyer. While Melanie had help, she became the hero in her own story. She could finally speak up, asked for help, and took herself out of harm's way. She attended therapy, found a new job, and began volunteering at a women's shelter. Melanie used what she learned to help others and became the hero to women just like her.

James was a practicing surgeon who'd become a medical doctor because he wanted to help people. At age forty, he was diagnosed with a familial tremor that meant he wouldn't be able to perform surgery. After receiving the depressing news, James didn't know what to do with his life.

He had a wife and two young children who looked up to him. James found it difficult to engage with them and soon lost sight of the future that he'd planned for his family.

When one of the doctors James played golf with suggested he consider going to counseling to cope with the sudden inability to perform surgery, he stopped talking to him. When his wife suggested the same thing, he locked himself in his home study. It wasn't until he overheard his children talking about making him a sandcastle so they could remember what his smile looked like, James realized he was the only one with the power to change his situation. His unhappiness had an unintended ripple effect, which made his wife and children unhappy, too.

James pulled out a notepad and began making lists. On one list, he jotted down all the career choices he'd contemplated when he was growing up, what he liked and didn't like about being a doctor, and his strengths and weaknesses. He made another list of what made him happy, and another of what he expected his future to look like.

James arranged all his lists in a row on the wall and focused on them for over a week. Later, he began making smaller lists and posting them beneath the original ones. He kept making smaller lists and posting them until he had a clear picture of where he wanted to be and what he wanted to do. James eventually whittled everything down to one final list and wrote it on one sheet of paper.

Before dinner one evening, he grabbed that list and joined his family at the kitchen table. He took ownership of his anger and apologized to his wife and children before announcing that while he could no longer perform surgery, he was going to use his talent and knowledge in a different way.

James presented his wife with the plan he'd mapped out. He was going to law school so he could represent doctors and during law school he planned to earn a living testifying as a medical expert. Once he was licensed to practice law, he could help people who'd been injured at the hands of doctors, as well as doctors who'd been wrongfully accused of medical malpractice. By doing so, he could use his knowledge and talents to find happiness, bring joy to others, and provide for his family.

James realized he was the only one who truly understood his own needs and desires. Therefore, he had to secure his own happiness before spreading joy to others or truly experiencing it himself. He needed to be the best version of himself, despite any setbacks, challenges, or uncertainty that came along. By following his plan and becoming a well-respected attorney, he became the hero in his own life, a hero to his family, and a hero to clients who were facing their biggest obstacles.

Being your own hero means having the courage to confront your negative thoughts with complete honesty. It means acknowledging your flaws, bad habits, and negative influences, and recognizing areas where you need to improve. Make a list and then look at it with fresh eyes a few hours, days, or weeks later. Respond to it with the same empathy and compassion you would offer to a struggling friend. Consider rephrasing negatives into positive statements. Identify honest mistakes, acknowledge the lessons learned, and anticipate the positive transformations that lie ahead. Look toward the greater character-building journey and find pleasure in the new experiences and challenges you engage with. Swap out harmful habits in favor of adopting good ones. Repeat this exercise as often as necessary to measure your personal growth and rid yourself of your villains. Embrace the benefits of being your own hero and inspiring others, even if all you do is lead by example and be the best version of yourself.

Final Thoughts . . .

Always remember that you are a gift with the ability to use and share your talents in a way that encourages, empowers, and bestows confidence.

Stand proud, embrace your identity, and honor the champion within you.

Set boundaries and exude valor.

Believe in yourself and trust your gut, even when others try to dissuade you.

Choose yourself because you are stronger, smarter, and skilled at everything important to you.

When you feel lost or confused, or like you're not in control, the simple act of recognizing and reflecting on your situation will guide you and help you regain a sense of control.

The only yardstick that measures your success is the one you create.

Keep moving forward despite failure, as valuable lessons pave the way to triumph.

Fear, failure, flop, and fiasco are the cornerstones on the foundation of success.

Be mindful of the impact you have on others and intentionally choose to be a positive influence.

Give yourself permission to live a joyful life full of purpose. Understand that both failures and successes are opportunities.

Living your truth inspires others to do the same.

Passion is the engine that drives us to our finest moments.

Transform silence into advocacy for change.

Maintain the acumen to flip mistakes and failure into wisdom and success.

The right decision is the one you can articulate, act upon, and take ownership of.

When you focus on what you have instead of what you lack, you maintain your power, control, and dignity.

A true hero knows when to help and when to sit back and let others be their own heroes.

www.ingramcontent.com/pod-product-compliance
Lightning Source LLC
Chambersburg PA
CBHW072156070526
44585CB00015B/1162